Confessing the Triune God

*W*esleyan Doctrine Series

The Wesleyan Doctrine Series seeks to reintroduce Christians in the Wesleyan tradition to the beauty of doctrine. The volumes in the series draw on the key sources for Wesleyan teaching: Scripture, Liturgy, Hymnody, the General Rules, the Articles of Religion and various Confessions. In this sense, it seeks to be distinctively Wesleyan. But it does this with a profound interest and respect for the unity and catholicity of Christ's body, the church, which is also distinctly Wesleyan. For this reason, the series supplements the Wesleyan tradition with the gifts of the church catholic, ancient, and contemporary. The Wesleyan tradition cannot survive without a genuine "Catholic Spirit." These volumes are intended for laity who have a holy desire to understand the faith they received at their baptism.

Editors:
Randy Cooper
Andrew Kinsey
D. Brent Laytham
D. Stephen Long

Confessing
the Triune God

DANIEL CASTELO

CASCADE *Books* · Eugene, Oregon

CONFESSING THE TRIUNE GOD

Wesleyan Doctrine Series 3

Copyright © 2014 Daniel Castelo. All rights reserved. Except for brief quotations in critical publications or reviews, no part of this book may be reproduced in any manner without prior written permission from the publisher. Write: Permissions, Wipf and Stock Publishers, 199 W. 8th Ave., Suite 3, Eugene, OR 97401.

Cascade Books
An Imprint of Wipf and Stock Publishers
199 W. 8th Ave., Suite 3
Eugene, OR 97401

www.wipfandstock.com

ISBN 13: 978-1-62032-504-9

Cataloging-in-Publication data:

Castelo, Daniel, 1978–

    Confessing the triune God / Daniel Castelo.

    xviii + 134 p. ; 23 cm. —Includes bibliographical references.

    Wesleyan Doctrine Series 3

    ISBN 13: 978-1-62032-504-9

    1. Theology, Doctrinal. 2. Christian life. I. Title. II. Series.

BT75.2 .C378 2014

Manufactured in the U.S.A.

To my colleagues
at the School of Theology
at Seattle Pacific University and Seminary

Contents

Acknowledgments

I wish to express my thanks to Prof. D. Stephen Long for the invitation to contribute to the "Wesleyan Doctrine" Series. Few people love the church and academy with heartfelt rigor the way Steve does, and it has been a pleasure working alongside him in ventures that attempt to help the church be more intentionally theological and the academy more intentionally ecclesial.

I wrote this book alongside the task of teaching a class on the Trinity to my undergraduate students at Seattle Pacific. Teaching an 8:00 A.M. class is not easy, but we had a wonderful time together, and they challenged and probed my work as it was emerging. Through this experience, writing, teaching, and thinking were distinct yet unified activities. I am grateful that the laboratory of the classroom helped make such confluences possible.

This book is dedicated to my colleagues at Seattle Pacific. As a collegium, they are people who love and fear God dispositionally and practically through the lives they lead and the work they do. I have grown as a thinker and believer in their midst, and I am grateful they have welcomed me as one of theirs. In terms of this project, Dean Strong, Frank Spina, Kevin Watson, and Rob Wall were important dialogue partners. Thanks to these and my many other colleagues. May the triune God richly bless you and grant you shalom.

Introduction

The topic of the Trinity is one that is plagued with assumptions about incomprehensibility. If there is one topic in Christianity that begs for illustration, it seems to be this one. We have all heard examples like the following: "The Trinity is like a tree: roots, trunk, branches," "the Trinity is like the different states of water: solid, liquid, gas," and (to take the recent favorite of a class of mine), "the Trinity is like an egg: shell, white, yolk."

Do these examples work to illustrate Trinitarianism? No, they do not. It is not because they are bad examples per se but misdirected: At their heart is the attempt to reconcile a mathematical or logical problem, namely, how something can be both three and one, but the Trinity is not primarily a logical problem. *What is at stake with the confession of the Trinity is not the reconciliation of numbers but rather the coherence and meaningfulness of what Christians wish to say about God and God's purposes in and for the world.* Throughout the centuries, the church has repeatedly maintained that the conception of God as triune is at the heart of what it means to be Christian.

This volume is written by a theologian and minister for the worshiping faithful, whether they are beginning theological students or devoted and curious church folk. The book stems from a commitment that theology ought to be pursued for the sake of the church as an act of worship to the triune God of Christian confession. In this sense, the volume seeks to function catechetically or instructively in faith matters at a time when the Western Christian church struggles to place demands upon itself. After all, becoming a member of the body of Christ is not necessarily the same act across epochs and contexts, including within our contemporary global scene. At different moments and places, to become a disciple of Christ has meant to undertake a life-risking identity. Pause for a second and consider the following: Being a Christian has been considered an act of rebellion or defiance in certain contexts. The identity has been serious enough to be viewed as threatening to the status quo or the ruling powers of a given era. Becoming a Christian has often not been an act of conformity or of soothing one's conscience but a life-altering (and potentially life-threatening) decision, one that people nevertheless have undertaken because what was at stake was that important. In this sense, catechesis was of utmost significance—people needed to know what they were getting into if they could die on account of it. Currently (and lamentably), it is questionable if in the north trans-Atlantic West Christian commitment is generally taken with the same degree of seriousness as in past epochs of Western history or in current situations one finds around the global South. Such difficulties are symptomatic not so much about Christianity but the way we in our contexts presently understand and appropriate it in our everyday lives.

One indicator of this state of affairs is the integrity and meaningfulness with which Christian speech is pursued and expressed. Do Western Christians really know what they are saying when they proclaim Jesus as "Lord"? Do they truly appreciate what it means to be saved and to live into God's inbreaking kingdom? Have Christian terms become so overused and domesticated that they fail to enchant and beckon the self who is employing them? If these questions generate less than satisfactory answers, then much of this malaise, I would argue, stems from faulty Christian God-talk. What I mean by the term "God-talk" is the names, imagery, and metaphors Christians use to describe the God they worship, and essential to Christian God-talk is the confession of the triune God. When Christians profess their belief in "God," they do so as a shorthand form of saying, "Father-Son-Holy Spirit." In other words, the confession of the Christian God as triune is not accidental to this God's identity but in fact essential. It is not clear if the typical Western Christian acknowledges and finds compelling this scandalous claim.

If we as Christians cannot maintain the integrity and meaningfulness of our God-talk, then there is little hope of understanding anything else that comes with Christian identity. Social justice, equality, inclusion, and a host of other topics that traffic as the heart of the gospel mean little apart from a vision and testimony of the God we serve and worship because essentially Christian identity is not about us but about God and what God has done for us (including creating, saving, and sanctifying us) as a God who is with us (Immanuel). It is because God is with us and so for us that Christians confess their God to be

Trinity, one who is beyond the bounds of infinity and yet closer to us than we are to ourselves. Such a claim is truly remarkable and awe-inspiring. In fact, given its shape and thrust, *the most interesting thing about Christianity is the triune God whom the church confesses, worships, loves, and obeys*. Nothing else compares.

The claim that the God of Christian worship is triune is a basic claim shared by the vast majority of the world's Christians, and yet that confession is one especially important to those fellowships that claim a Wesleyan heritage. In the ministries, thought, prose, and poetry of the brothers Wesley and their Methodist associates and progeny, the dogma or teaching of the Trinity has been central to all else that is. A quick perusal of Wesleyan and Methodist denominational bodies proves the point. As Ted Campbell has noted, four major Methodist denominations (the African Methodist Episcopal [AME] Church, the African Methodist Episcopal Zion [AME Zion] Church, the Christian Methodist Episcopal [CME] Church, and the United Methodist Church [UMC]) share a doctrinal heritage that includes the "Twenty-five Articles of Religion" (1784). And related to the present study, these articles begin with an elaboration of the Trinity: "There is but one living and true God, everlasting, without body or parts, of infinite power, wisdom, and goodness; the maker and preserver of all things, both visible and invisible. And in unity of this Godhead there are three persons, of one substance, power, and eternity—the Father, the Son, and the Holy Ghost."[1] Also, the Free Methodist Church straightaway begins its doctrinal commitments with an article on the Trinity: "There is but

1. Campbell, *Methodist Doctrine*, 114.

one living and true God, the maker and preserver of all things. And in the unity of this Godhead there are three persons: the Father, the Son, and the Holy Spirit. These three are one in eternity, deity, and purpose; everlasting, of infinite power, wisdom, and goodness."[2] In its "Articles of Religion," the Wesleyan Church says much of the same: "We believe in the one living and true God, both holy and loving, eternal, unlimited in power, wisdom and goodness, the Creator and Preserver of all things. Within this unity there are three persons of one essential nature, power and eternity—the Father, the Son and the Holy Spirit,"[3] and following this article are additional sections that treat of each of the triune persons. These and many other Methodist and Wesleyan fellowships relate explicitly the importance of faith in the Trinity through their doctrinal statements and confessions of faith.

Given the prominence of Trinitarianism within this subtradition of Christianity, the present text hopes to draw from the riches of the Wesleyan ethos as one feature constituting a more general conversation about the church's confession of the triune God. Such an orientation is supported by the assumption that a vital way to see the Trinity's importance is to locate the topic within the life and history of a particular ecclesial tradition. For this reason, this work seeks to bring the Wesleyan testimony to the work of surveying the shape of Trinitarianism within the life and practice of those who gather, pray, baptize, and celebrate in the name of the Father, Son, and Holy Spirit.

2. See http://fmcusa.org/uniquelyfm/doctrine.

3. See http://www.wesleyan.org/beliefs#part1.

Comments

Daniel Castelo's commentary on the Trinity provides a wonderful opportunity for persons and groups to explore a sometimes difficult teaching in the life of the church. Daniel's summary of the Trinity builds on solid historical and ecumenical foundations while also drawing out the distinctive features of Wesleyan and Methodist insights.

The following discussion questions are meant to assist readers in Daniel's exploration of the Trinity. They have been created to help persons and churches with the ongoing conversation the church has been having through the centuries and to point out the kind of speech we use in making our common confession. While the current set of questions do not exhaust all the angles of the Trinity, they will hopefully instigate further discussion, if not, action in the church. This present commentary is one of several commentaries in the Wesleyan Doctrine Series designed to engage the church in spiritual formation and theological education and instruction.

Andrew Kinsey

Questions for Consideration

1. What is at stake with confession of the Trinity? Share how "coherence" and "meaningfulness" relate to the ways we speak of God's purposes and identity.

2. What is suggested by the term "God-talk"? What are the consequences of faulty "God-talk" in the life of the church?

3. How is the confession of the Trinity considered essential to the church's worship and to the church's mission?

4. Share how important the Trinity is to Christians in the various Wesleyan traditions and how the Trinity may serve to unite Christians in terms of faith and practice.

5. Why learn about the Holy Trinity? What difference does the Trinity make to the church's mission and in our daily lives?

one

Coming to Terms
with the *Christian* God

In his classic *Mere Christianity*, C. S. Lewis entertains a train of thought, a theo-logic that moves from general to particular claims. He appeals to a "Law of Human Nature," a sense of morality that, broadly speaking, all humans assume and yet by their own acknowledgment fail to fulfill in all of its details. Features of this law would include decency, honesty, fairness, and the like. This law is a clue for Lewis of "something else" behind it, specifically a source of this law since it would appear that humans have not simply and haphazardly come up with it, given its universal (rather than sporadic) manifestation within the human experience. According to Lewis, this source would seem to be more akin to a "mind" than to a "thing" since the law is prescriptive rather than descriptive. As Lewis remarks, "I think we have to assume it is more like a mind than it is like anything else we know—because after all the only other thing we know is matter and you can hardly imagine a bit of matter giving instructions."[1]

1. *Mere Christianity*, 31.

Lewis' focus at this point of his argument is on this law, although he mentions another possible evidence for this "mind," namely, the universe and its character as ordered, beautiful, and good. These two appeals have a specific history; thinkers have long considered them as suggestions for the possible existence of a being behind all that we know.[2] However contentious the claim, some have resorted to calling them indicators or even "proofs" for the existence of a divine being.

It is important to note that ruminations like Lewis' do point to a kind of theism, a general sense that some kind of transcendent being exists; however, *these claims do not go far enough to be called "Christian" quite yet.* Lewis admits this much, and one has to be clear about the matter when one ventures into this kind of speculative task. The vast majority of the world has been and continues to be, to use Lewis' nomenclature, "religious" as opposed to "materialist."[3] Many people today, even in the pluralist and secularist societies of the West, claim that some kind of divinity exists. In fact, religious devotion—rather than phasing out and dying as certain prognosticators assumed would happen in the 1960s—has actually increased significantly worldwide over the last decades. Therefore, belief in a "higher power" is not that remarkable. By all means, this situation is not lamentable from a Christian perspective, but a claim of belief in some kind of divinity is not that exceptional. The vast majority of people on this planet are already there. Secularists,

2. For instance, these two phenomena inspired awe and reverence for Immanuel Kant, as noted toward the end of the *Critique of Practical Reason*.

3. *Mere Christianity*, 28–29.

thoroughgoing materialists, and atheists are in the deep minority across the globe.

Many Christians think this affirmation of some kind of mind behind the universe is enough to be Christian, but it is unequivocally not. Truth be told, the distance between this generalized theism and the Christian God is vast indeed. Christians affirm this generalized theistic logic to be sure, but so do Jews, Muslims, and others. Such reasoning is not enough to speak of the Christian God, and in and of themselves, these thought-forms are not particularly Christian.

Theism Is Not Necessarily Christian

At this point, one temptation that presents itself to Christians and other religiously minded individuals is to assume the sufficiency of a generalized theism. People tend to believe that because the term *god* is so prevalent the idea is a workable and shared starting point for subsequent interchange. Because of convenience, the urgency to make a connection with others, or some other reason, many find it tempting to say, "We all worship the same god because we can all agree that there is something or someone behind the order of the universe and the moral law. Our paths may be different, but the destination is the same." *If only the matter were so simple.* We have to stop and ask ourselves: Why do we find such thinking and reasoning desirable? Why are we prone to value and seek generalization so much? Have Christians always operated this way? Why and in what manner do we presently privilege this approach? More importantly: What does such

Not that simple

3

a framing allow us to do, and what gaps does it create? What does it achieve that we find beneficial and desirable, and are such benefits and desires fulfilled at a cost?[4]

I tend to label this alternative toward generalization a "temptation" because within our pluralistic context, it makes a lot of sense and it is quite compelling to say, "You do it your way, I'll do it my way, and we are both not wrong; in fact, we are really doing the same thing, only differently." In other words, this kind of thinking and speaking is appealing so as to avoid marking differences or any kind of normative claims, ones that imply that someone is "right" and the other is "wrong." We tend to think that normativity creates conflict and that it promotes "closed-mindedness" and "intolerance." For instance, in the particular case of Christians, they are often portrayed by the popular media as "judgmental" and "bigoted" because they are said to think their way is the only way. Rather than accommodating difference, Christians are often cast as those who think of themselves as going to heaven and others who do not agree with them as going to hell. Such a broad depiction of Christians (however accurate on a case-by-case basis) represents the quintessential antitype to today's flourishing and engaged citizen, one who is "open-minded" and "tolerant" to diversity. Under such arrangements, the private-public dichotomy runs ram-

---

4. I want to be clear in saying that a conversation on the basis of a generalized theism can in some sense be fruitful (as Lewis entertains for a time in *Mere Christianity*); however, I am arguing against the *privileging* of a generalized theism for Christians. This privileging not only makes this intimation of the divine a starting point but potentially also morphs it into an all-sufficient construct and/or criterion-set for other theistic claims and goals. For instance, how important are the Bible and the church if a generalized theism is all we need?

pant, and again, morality—when understood as implying particular ways of living in the world based on construals of what is best—is assumed to function properly in the private realm of one's life so as to not be a stumbling block or an affront to public engagement. Particularity and normativity are thus viewed as divisive; generalizability and toleration (the latter trafficking as self-proclaimed "non-judgmentalism") are enlightened and progressive.

But let us push further. Normative claims are not simply about who is "right" and who is "wrong." On the contrary, they imply a broader vision about what is desirable and true. In other words, they suggest a particular way to live, and everyone assumes these in some way. There is no escaping these kinds of concerns because we are already active and living in the world. Given that we live, interact, and make decisions as a by-product of simply existing, we assume quite a bit about what is good and worth pursuing, whether we explicitly claim so or not. For instance, some of the most closed-minded people in our society are those who defiantly and nonnegotiably hold to an account of "open-mindedness." Anything that does not fit within their account of what is "reasonable" is deemed suspect, stupid, and antiquated. It is hard to gain a hearing with an "open-minded" person if one is already deemed by such a person to be "closed-minded." The point is that *no one is thoroughly "open-minded." Everybody draws the line somewhere, and such is an inevitable consequence of being human.*

A generalized theism "keeps things simple" by not forcing us to come to terms with how we already answer the question, what are we living for? It helps perpetuate the standard morality of our society ("You do it your way, and I'll do it my way")—the one that we imbibe and are conditioned by since birth—by not exposing its assumptions for questioning. One should note, however, that a generalized theism is an impoverished theism; it is not enough by which to order one's life because it does not place demands or offer a thoroughgoing account of what is good, beautiful, and true. The closest one can approximate to such an account through a generalized theism is an elaboration of the moral law (as Lewis does in *Mere Christianity*), and often this takes the shape of the Golden Rule, which has confirmation in Scripture (Matt 7:12; Luke 6:31).

But can a good and happy life be pursued according to the Golden Rule? The Golden Rule may help cultivate a modicum of tolerance, respect, and empathy, but present within the Golden Rule are different levels of ambiguity. For instance, why do unto others as we would have them do unto us? What do we want from others, and are these desires justified? Why is this outlook mandated, and are people simply compelled by the reasonableness of this "ought"? Can the Golden Rule be cast in selfish terms? What is the end, purpose, or by-product of following this rule? These questions show the Golden Rule to be a secondary claim, one that requires a primary account of the good. The Golden Rule does not give an account of the integrity and complexity of both human persons and their activities, nor does it take into account what might promote and impede human flourishing. When people assume that the Golden Rule is an account of the good, moral discourse barely lifts off the ground. An indication of this embryonic state is a particular corruption of the Golden Rule quite prevalent in public discourse: "Do *if we don't talk about it, nothing will ever get solved!*

what you want to do as along as it doesn't get in the way of what I want to do." This "common morality" is not a productive way to order, sustain, or cultivate either individual or communal life. This moral sensibility does not address the more fundamental queries: *And what should we want to do?* How are we to live and die in such a fashion that we can be satisfied with our lives? What does a good human life look like? Should life be more than about us, and if so, how and why?

not good

Contemporary Christians face a lot of pressure to boil down their beliefs to the so-called essentials in a pluralist, secular culture that does not understand or tolerate legitimate religious differences. For a society that values toleration as a key civic virtue, ours is pretty intolerant of religious particularity (especially if such particularity is eccentric and runs counter to popular ideals and practices), since at its core secular society finds religious belief to be impractical and to some extent nonsensical. As noted above, for many years religious scholars were predicting the end of religious faith because, it was assumed, modernity would make religious commitment implausible and so impossible. For those who are not willing to take the risk of being marginalized by a secular status quo for their faith commitments, a generalized theism is a helpful "middle option." But in choosing this possibility, people succumb to some serious risks, ones that cut to the heart of a viable and vital Christian life.

First, if a generalized theism and the supposed "respectable" Christianity that issues from it are realized among those seeking to maintain their religious identity, a number of Christian practices that do not make sense to the broader culture (pacifism, chastity, singleness, forgiveness, hospitality, and a host of others) can be brushed to the side because they have no basis on which to stand. In other words, *a generalized theism is rarely counter-cultural and costly*. Often the quest for "essentials" is not for the sake of preserving the basics as much as identifying the minimums for the sake of convenience; that is to say, this strategy helps one seek the lowest common denominator for the sake of having the greatest relevance and so appeal. Such a pursuit, however, does not necessarily lead to vitality, renewal, and flourishing. Quite the contrary, this process tames any form of eccentricity and sacrifice because it fits so well within what is considered plausible, rational, and acceptable in the public realm. Put bluntly, a generalized theism does not require or foster changed or transformed lives; instead, a generalized theism facilitates and perpetuates "life as usual." But let us be clear: "Life as usual" is not the "good news" of the gospel or the life made possible by Jesus and the Spirit.

Second, many Christian beliefs, particularly those associated with Israel and Jesus, have no warrants within the prolonged perpetuation of a generalized theism. Generalization is totalizing; it makes little room for particularity. If sustained, generalization usually out-narrates, explains away, and brushes aside particularity as incidental and so inconsequential. If left unchecked, generalization destroys some of the most basic features of Christian identity. Anything that does not conform to its standards is deemed nonsensical and so pushed to the side. On such a list would be a number of vital Christian claims, including the Christian confession of the triune God.

Does Scripture Support a Generalized Theism?

But before we get too ahead of ourselves, it would be worth asking: Does Scripture support a generalized theism? One potential place for negotiating this question is the depiction of Paul in Athens (Acts 17:16–34). Essentially, Acts reports Paul as saying that the "unknown god" worshiped by the Athenians is the God of Jesus Christ. The appeal here is to the general side of things, and maybe folks who are looking for biblical support for generalized theism would find something here to bolster their outlook.

As a way of orienting our approach to this passage, let us recall that Paul makes this claim as a Jesus-following Jew. He began in Athens at the synagogue, and as he was arguing with Jews and others, Stoic and Epicurean thinkers came along and *on the basis of his new teaching about Jesus and the resurrection* (v. 18) took him to the Areopagus. Paul proceeds to relate the "unknown god" to a specific entity, one who "from one ancestor" made all nations. He speaks generally but consistently with an eye to particularity, ending, in verse 31, with these words: "He has fixed a day on which he will have the world judged in righteousness by a man whom he has appointed, and of this he has given assurance to all by raising him from the dead." With the claim of resurrection, Paul ends where it started for him personally, namely, the resurrected Jesus, at which point it seems his venture with the Athenians was met with scoffing and deferral.

It is this confessional stance that makes Paul's move intelligible. What appears on the surface as possible support for a generalized theism is actually a set of claims that is viable due to something else. This passage, as with the general scope of Scripture, points to the claim that Christianity operates out of what is often deemed today a *scandalous particularity*. Christian speech and thought may make the move toward generalization as a way of establishing workable relationships with others, but its meaningfulness and coherence *require* particularity. There is no escaping that, according to Christian confession, the triune God has revealed Godself to a particular people (Israel) and through a particular person (Jesus of Nazareth). Furthermore, particularity relates to the life that the term *Christian* is to instantiate. Jesus makes a direct call to his disciples ("Follow me" [Matt 4:19; Mark 1:17]), and his thrice-repeated question to Peter ("Do you love me?" [John 21:15–17]) is pointed and direct in relation to how Peter is disposed to this particular, resurrected person, his rabbi of three years. Little in terms of tame, conveniently ambiguous, and generalized claims is at play here, both in relation to the divine self-presentation and the call to discipleship.

Particularity as a Starting Point

The argument being pursued here is specific and should not be taken to extremes. As noted above, it could be the case that people, irrespective of religious persuasion, could have some sense of the divine. *On Christian terms*, such an intuition is viable in that all creatures are created by God and all humans reflect the divine image in some way. Under one frame of consideration, one could say that all have the Spirit of God because all have life. Nevertheless, Christians generally have not found these tendencies to be enough, not just in terms of "who's saved and who's not" but also (and more pressingly) in regard to living in the fullness of truth. At the heart of the Christian life are very particular claims about a particular God, who does particular things in history for particular ends. And as such, the claims made upon us as would-be followers of this God are demanding—and so particular as well.

John Wesley was aware of the gravity of these differences. In his sermon "The Almost Christian," he draws a distinction between the "almost" and "altogether" Christian. On first blush, what he associates with an "almost Christian" is quite a bit: He includes "heathen honesty," justice, fairness, truth-telling, and a host of other actions and dispositions that ancient pagan authors valued and lauded.[5] Wesley even goes so far as to say that being an "almost Christian" involves a "form of godliness"! With these high demands for the "almost Christian," what did Wesley associate with the "altogether Christian"? These marks are precisely dispositions and attitudes that are not compatible with the privileging of a generalized theism. Among these dispositions one can find the chief feature of the law, namely, loving God. Drawing upon and echoing key biblical passages, Wesley remarks that the "altogether Christian" has "'his delight . . . in the Lord,' *his* Lord and his all, to whom 'in everything he giveth thanks.' All *his* 'desire is unto God, and to the remembrance of his name' . . . Indeed, what can he desire beside God?"[6] In pursuing the point of desire, Wesley subsequently raises and poses questions *directly* to his hearers and readers: "Is the love of God shed abroad in your heart? Can you cry out, 'My God and my all'? Do

5. "The Almost Christian," 131–32.

6. Ibid., 137 (emphasis in original).

you desire nothing but him? Are you happy in God? Is he your glory, your delight, your crown of rejoicing?"[7] These traits of the "altogether Christian" suggest that faith in the Christian God is costly and all-consuming, not only in the negative sense of giving up things for God but also positively in the sense of delighting and enjoying God's very self.

And just to drive the point further that the Christian God is not a generalized deity, Wesley continues: "Yea, dost thou believe that Christ loved *thee*, and gave himself for thee? Hast thou faith in his blood? . . . And doth his Spirit bear witness with *thy* spirit, that thou art a child of God?"[8] This particular God has done particular things on behalf of us as particular entities so that in turn this God can demand particular things from us. The appropriation of this transformative and life-altering work is particular, as is the manner by which one lives into that work and shows gratitude and praise for it.

Particularity Matters

As one can see, and by way of concluding the point, the particularity of religious claims is directly tied to the relevance and significance of those claims as they take shape in specific lives. In other words, the specificity of a God-grammar directly influences and shapes Christian commitment. An operative vision of who God is and what God has done is the bedrock for an understanding of what the Christian life is and can be. Without a vibrant

7. Ibid., 140–41.
8. Ibid., 141 (emphasis in original).

apprehension of the God of Christian confession, the life that marks itself as a follower of this God will inevitably falter as a result. Despite the tension that may exist as to which passage reflects summarily the law and the prophets (for instance, Matt 7:12 or 22:40), the Wesleyan emphasis is very clear: The Great Love Commandments, and not just the Golden Rule, constitute the chief motivation and end of the community of Christ-followers. If a people were to live into these commandments, nothing would be costlier and yet more life-giving all at once.

you have to be willing to give up EVERYTHING to be willing

Questions for Consideration

1. How are C. S. Lewis' ruminations about "generalized theism" helpful? What are the limitations to, or the problems with, the claims of "generalized theism" versus the church's confession of the Holy Trinity? What are the temptations to revert to generalized theism?

2. What is the myth of a generalized theism? Is it as "open" to other theological claims as it purports to be? Share some of the risks associated with generalized theism. How does generalized theism move in the direction of totalizing speech about God?

3. How does the story of the Apostle Paul in Acts help clarify the theological significance of the "scandalous particularity" of the gospel? Why do meaningfulness and coherence with the church's God-talk require particularity? Can Christians escape such "scandalous," "particular" speech? Explain.

4. How does John Wesley's distinction between the "almost" and "altogether" Christian help differentiate between generalized forms of theism and particular speech claims of the Trinity? What are the insights to such a distinction? Are they useful?

5. How is our "specific God-grammar" with respect to the church's confession of the Trinity to directly influence and shape Christian discipleship? What are the consequences of speaking of God poorly or incorrectly in worship? In the public square?

two

Trinitarianism as a Mechanism of Coherence

In the last chapter we considered how a generalized theism is largely inconsonant with Christian belief. At the heart of Christianity are claims of particularity, both regarding who God is and what God has done for us. The shape of this particularity has been scandalous to many moderns who believe that the most important, relevant, and safest way to deal with religious belief is to pursue generalizability.

Friedrich Schleiermacher, often called the father of modern or liberal theology, strove toward this generalizability. He did so through the aspect of experience, one that he called the feeling of "absolute dependence." In his view, this feeling marked all religious sentiment and could be generalizable in degrees regardless of context or particularity. It is no wonder then that he found the dogma or teaching of the Trinity to be challenging given his outlook. In his famous volume on Christian teaching, he remarked, "But this doctrine [of the Trinity] itself, as ecclesiastically framed, is not an immediate utterance concerning the Christian self-consciousness, but only a combination of several such utterances."[1] Schleiermacher's concern is that the dogma of the Trinity is not experientially and so immediately accessible; one has to be taught so as to conclude deliberatively that God is triune. This reality suggests the inherent speculative nature of Trinitarian speech. Without teachers and left to their own, Christians would not necessarily come to believe in the Trinity as this teaching has been framed through church tradition, and such dependence takes away from Trinitarianism's generalizability and so (in Schleiermacher's mind) the long-term value of its traditional forms. The case of Schleiermacher is simply symptomatic of a broader condition: For moderns, generalizability is viewed as the only way forward amidst competing and contradictory claims. The general is seen as an aid to build peace and mutual understanding, and the particular is suspiciously viewed as speculative, a matter of personal taste, and divisive.

A basic problem, however, with this modern privileging of generalizability is that it operates out of a profound ignorance and shortsightedness regarding how many, if not most, people pursue and live out their religious commitments. As Stephen Prothero notes, "Pretending that the world's religions are the same does not make our world safer. Like all forms of ignorance, it makes our

1. *Christian Faith*, 738. One of the most basic utterances for Schleiermacher would be "the doctrine of the union of the Divine Essence with human nature, both in the personality of Christ and in the common Spirit of the Church," for "therewith the whole view of Christianity set forth in our Church stands and falls" (ibid.).

world more dangerous."[2] The antidote to this ignorance is to take religious difference seriously. Religious particularities matter for the sake of the integrity and practice of religious commitments. The assumption that all religions and all depictions about a "higher entity" are ultimately different expressions of the same thing perpetuates a specific kind of violence upon religious commitments, one that is both totalizing and dismissive.

Schleiermacher's views do have a certain appeal, however, because they do point to a reality with which one must wrestle: If left alone to pray and read the Bible, a person coming to Christian faith would not come to conclude that God's life and being can be specifically characterized as "one essence eternally subsisting as three persons." Nevertheless, Christians throughout history have come to use this kind of language and to extend its logic for very good reasons, and those reasons matter to Christians as they try to be faithful and consistent in their speech about the Christian God they confess and worship.

The Two Layers of Particularity

As a way of making a case for the way Christians have historically thought about the triune God, one must account for two important levels of particularity. One layer is Israel, the other is Jesus. From Christianity's perspective, the two require one another in different ways. On one side of the dynamic, Christians hold that Jesus is Israel's Messiah, that the promises of "the One to come"

2. Prothero, *God Is Not One*, 4.

17

are fulfilled in the life of this man. For this reason, people sometimes speak of the "Christ-event," for the coming of Christ is for Christians a culminating moment in the covenant relationship between God and Israel. From another angle, Christians read and make sense of the works of God in the Old Testament *through* Jesus, for Jesus represents to Christians the most concrete and reliable expression of God's character. This last point suggests that Christians always begin and end with Christ when negotiating and developing their understanding of God generally and their God-talk particularly. Israel preceded and so anticipated Jesus historically, yet Jesus the Christ provides Christians with the theological lens to interpret the sum of God's work as manifest in the life of Israel and the church. All of this is to say that even at these levels of particularity further nuancing and qualification are required. To understand Jesus one needs a workable sense of the law's purposes and ends so that its fulfillment in Jesus may be generative and satisfying at the theological level. At the same time, a parting of ways between Judaism and Christianity has taken place in that Christians believe that Jesus is the anticipated Messiah foretold in Israel's history. In light of this rupture, the levels of particularity have to be considered in terms of their inner-workings and emphases within the theological task.

Israel

In regard to the first level of particularity outlined above, Jews believe that of all the peoples of the world, the one true God has revealed Godself to them. But this conviction is not simply cognitive; it involves a commitment and a promise—in sum, a covenant: "Go from your country and your kindred and your father's house to the land that I will show you. I will make of you a great nation, and I will bless you, and make your name great, so that you will be a blessing. I will bless those who bless you, and the one who curses you I will curse; and in you all the families of the earth shall be blessed" (Gen 12:1–3).

Specifically as Paul negotiates this particularity in the Epistle to the Romans, the promise made to Israel was not meant to be simply for this nation. Rather than reductive, this covenant was to be expansive, again from the particular to the more general: "For this reason it depends on faith, in order that the promise may rest on grace and be guaranteed to all his descendants, not only to the adherents of the law but also to those who share the faith of Abraham" (Rom 4:16). And Paul's understanding here is that those who share this faith are those "who believe in him who raised Jesus our Lord from the dead" (Rom 4:24). What God was doing through Israel was meant to be a blessing to the nations of the earth. But this movement from particularity to generality should not take away from what has to be attended to in terms of particularity. Essentially, God shows God's character over time within the covenant relationship God establishes with Israel. And so, rather than being the god of generalized theism, the God of the Abrahamic covenant has a name, character attributes, desires, and purposes because this God has willed to have a history with this particular people. Within the Jewish mindset the implications are generalizable ("The God who made the world and everything in it, he who is Lord of heaven and earth"

[Acts 17:24]), yet they take shape within the particular ("God also said to Moses, 'Thus you shall say to the Israelites, "YHWH,[3] the God of your ancestors, the God of Abraham, the God of Isaac, and the God of Jacob, has sent me to you": This is my name forever, and this is my title for all generations'" [Exod 3:15]).

Because of these claims, Jews have historically elevated the Shema as one of the most important passages of Scripture for their God-talk: "Hear, O Israel: YHWH is our God, YHWH alone" (Deut 6:4). This verse and others have contributed to Judaism being recognized as a "monotheistic" religion. Jewish monotheism has a number of features, but two in particular are worth pressing. Of high importance is the observation that biblical monotheism suggests that YHWH is preeminently above all other deities. As plenty of Old Testament passages show, other deities, ones associated with Israel's neighbors and enemies, are assumed by Scripture to exist. Nevertheless, YHWH is unquestionably and persistently hailed as superior to them. For instance, Elijah challenged the prophets of Baal, and once bulls were chosen and placed on an altar, a contest involving divine superiority ensued: "Then you call on the name of your god and I [Elijah] will call on the name of YHWH; the god who answers by fire is indeed God" (1 Kgs 18:24). The character of Scripture's witness should mark biblical monotheism as first and foremost

3. Readers should know, if they are unfamiliar with the details, that the name revealed to Moses in Exod 3 is a variant of the verb "to be," and it can be translated as "I am who I am" or "I will be who I will be." Jews typically do not pronounce this name and use other possibilities to communicate it (for instance, *Adonai*), and often English translations recognize the uniqueness of this name by rendering "Lord" in small caps as its equivalent.

a claim directed to secure YHWH's preeminence among other gods.

Given the etymology of the word, many have taken monotheism to imply that the God of Jewish confession is also numerically one. This aspect of monotheism is a bit more complicated. Not only is one of the titles for God plural in the Old Testament (*Elohim*), but more pressingly, the divine is related in the Old Testament in a number of ways that suggest a certain understanding or accommodation toward multiplicity. God's Word, God's Spirit, God's Wisdom, as well as God's messengers all suggest both a unity and diversity in God's self-presentation within Israel's sacred texts. Of course, rank-and-file Jews do not assume something like a Trinitarian understanding in their vision of who YHWH is and what YHWH is like, but one should not allow the etymology of a term such as *monotheism* to overdetermine what is a complicated testimony within Israel's scriptures. The numerical aspect of monotheism should thus be bracketed or at least subsumed under the more primary consideration of preeminence, given the different ways God reveals Godself in Scripture.

Jesus: Preliminary Considerations

The second and most pressing layer of particularity associated with Christian God-talk involves Jesus. This first-century Nazarene was born a Jew, and his Jewishness was deeply integral to his identity, both historical and theological. In this sense, Jesus' followers participate in the promise of which Jesus is the fulfillment. Followers of

Jesus are devoted disciples of a Jewish teacher; they claim Abraham as "their father"; and they believe themselves to be part of a covenant history. Many things distinguish Christians from Jews, but, as mentioned above, what is a major stumbling block between the two is that Christians believe Jesus is the long-awaited Messiah promised in the Jewish scriptures. For Christians, he is the prophet like Moses (Deut 18:15–22), the Suffering Servant (Isa 52:13— 53:12), a priest according to the order of Melchizedek (Ps 110:4), and the Son of Man, the king whose dominion is everlasting (Dan 7:14).

But the difference between Jews and Christians goes deeper than simply one group believing Jesus is the Messiah and the other refusing the point. Christians have moved to reconsider and reconstrue the role of Messiah as embodied by Jesus since he is, Christians will contend, not simply a figure like Aaron, Moses, David, Elijah, and others. The fundamental Christian claim is that Jesus is Lord and Savior, and such remarks increase the pressure[4] of the divine-human interface, particularly as it relates both to Jesus' relationship to YHWH[5] (Israel's God and Jesus' Father) and the place of Jesus' disciples within the Abrahamic covenant.

4. I am indebted to C. Kavin Rowe and his many works for the helpful language of "pressure" when considering these themes; see, for instance, "Biblical Pressure and Trinitarian Hermeneutics." He himself will attribute this language on occasion to Brevard Childs.

5. On this point, see the highly generative article by David Yeago, "The New Testament and the Nicene Dogma," as well as Hurtado, *One God, One Lord*.

Jesus' Identity

So, who was Jesus? Many people have a high regard for Jesus as a good person and a sound moral teacher. But this assessment requires a certain hermeneutical self-privileging because it does not take Jesus for what he has come to mean for Christians throughout the centuries. Jesus' goal was not to be a good moral teacher, much less "a really nice guy." Christians esteem Jesus not simply because he was wise, loving, and concerned for people on the margins. The history of Jesus-interpretation is plagued by efforts to fit his life into what many sense is a palatable, and so tame, form. As a result, people pick and choose those parts of his life and teachings that can "work" or "fit" such forms and conveniently avoid those that do not. got to read the context

These efforts are not entirely implausible because Jesus' identity is a complicated matter, as Scripture itself will attest. In terms of the fourfold gospel testimony, the identity of Jesus is such a pivotal concern that at times it drives the narrative plotline. For instance, the Gospel of Mark progresses in large part through developments and illuminations surrounding Jesus' identity. Whereas the demons apparently knew early on who he was (1:24, 34; 3:11; 5:7), the scribes were puzzled because he was claiming to forgive sins (2:7), his disciples were in awe because he controlled the natural elements (4:41), and his fellow Nazarenes dismissed him as simply a commoner they knew all too well (6:3). In Mark, no scarcity of theories exists related to Jesus' identity (6:14–16; 8:28), and although Peter's confession hits the mark (8:29), the matter reaches a heightened form in Jesus' trial, both before the temple authorities, when the high priest asks him, "'Are you the Messiah, the Son of the Blessed One?'" (14:61), and later before Pilate, who asks him if he was the king of the Jews (15:2).

Of incalculable consequence for the understanding of Jesus' identity are the developments associated with his post-resurrection appearances. When Mary Magdalene and Jesus' mother come to the empty tomb and hear the words from the angel, they hurry to tell his disciples, when unexpectedly Jesus meets them on the way. What was their reaction? "And they came to him, took hold of his feet, and *worshiped* him" (Matt 28:9, emphasis added). Later within the same chapter, one sees that when the disciples gathered together on a mountain and in turn beheld him, they too worshiped him (Matt 28:17). The Gospel of Luke also makes the point of emphasizing the worship of the resurrected Jesus (24:52). In other words, the post-resurrected Jesus was worshiped by early Christians because of their belief that "the God of Israel [had] *identified* himself with the particular human being, Jesus of Nazareth."[6] Of course, such a move was theologically scandalous in Judaism; the act of worshiping Jesus and its implications for Jewish theology needed sustained and deliberate consideration so as not to fall into incoherence and/or Jewish apostasy.

6. Yeago, "New Testament and the Nicene Dogma," 89 (emphasis in original).

The Two Instantiating Claims of Trinitarianism

The practice by early Christians of worshiping Jesus led to a conundrum. On the one hand, early Christians held to monotheism as it was understood in Judaism, both in terms of the Shema as well as the first commandment: "You shall have no other gods before me" (Exod 20:3). And yet, these early believers were *worshiping Jesus*, thereby functionally at least making him divine. Obviously, these two claims stand in tension with one another. Either YHWH, Jesus' Father, is preeminently God and Jesus is somehow subordinate, or traditional Jewish monotheism is in need of reconstrual given the claims and practices of early Christians. What the church eventually decided was that "Jesus [was to be] defined with reference to God [YHWH] and God [YHWH] [was to be] (re)defined with reference to Jesus as unique agent of God's revealing and redemptive purposes."[7]

Before moving ahead of ourselves, let us register a couple of points that follow from this logic. First, Christian Trinitarianism is a product of the beliefs and practices associated with Jesus the Christ and their impact on how the church came to confess and believe in the God of Israel. Naturally, it is hypothetical and speculative to suggest how things could have been otherwise apart from Jesus, but this much is clear in terms of the logical implications: Jesus—both his life (beginning with the incarnation) and what his followers made of him—occasioned and shaped Trinitarian considerations in Christian reflection. In other words, *without Jesus, there would not be Christian Trinitarianism as we understand*

7. Hurtado, "Monotheism," 520.

it today. It is because of Jesus that Christians have moved to take multiplicity seriously as part of the divine life.[8] The work of YHWH and the work of Jesus are so closely aligned in the New Testament (both in terms of how Jesus is portrayed and the way NT writers interpreted the OT) that one cannot help but sense a "binitarian" shape to Christian God-talk emerging in the early period of the church's existence, both through its practices and its catechetical and scriptural materials.

This point marks a second matter for consideration, namely that the Christian confession of the triune God is bound up with revelational claims. These convictions, in other words, are garnered from what Christians believe to be the manner of God's self-presentation within history. Christian belief in the Trinity is not strictly speculative and abstract. People did not simply come up with the idea of the Trinity in order to press the point that God is unfathomable or mysterious; rather, Christian Trinitarianism issues from the struggle of Jesus-following Jews and Gentiles to make sense of God's self-presentation in Jesus as this relates to Israel's testimony and the significance they see Jesus having for cosmic salvation history.

Put succinctly, the Christian confession of the triune God is the church's attempt to make sense of 1) Jewish monotheism and 2) the worship (and so the identity) of Jesus. Trinitarian dogma or teaching is a result of the

8. As Geoffrey Wainwright has remarked, "The Incarnation—understood to include the whole life and destiny of Jesus—is the trigger for belief in the Triune God and the development of Trinitarian doctrine. If there was no Incarnation, then the doctrine of the Trinity falls" ("Doctrine of the Trinity," 124).

church's self-attentive task of making sense of all that it wishes to say about YHWH in light of Jesus. The efforts to maintain these claims have not always been clear, consistent, or fully developed, but these were the concerns operating in the background that eventually led to formal clarifications about such matters. The end results were vastly important since Trinitarian teaching affirms both promise and fulfillment, continuity of history and discontinuity of expectation, as well as unity in action and distinction in personhood within the divine life itself.

The Orthodoxy of Wesleyan Theology

Wesleyan theology for the most part has followed the patterns of assuming rather than expounding a Trinitarian logic with conceptual and definitional rigor. For instance, in his only sermon nominally devoted to the topic, John Wesley was keen to emphasize the Trinity's mystery as well as the pitfalls of explanation when the theme is broached.[9] Although the sermon is the only one of its kind in Wesley's corpus, one should not assume that Wesley was only nominally Trinitarian. In addition to the occasional triadic reference, Wesley's works depend upon the logic of the Son and the Spirit operating within the economy to the glory of the Father. Wesleyan theological distinctives—including the new birth, assurance, transformation, and others—require a Trinitarian sensibility for their cogency. The following quote is typical of this Trinitarian requirement: "This eternal life then commences when it pleases the Father to reveal his Son in our

9. See "On the Trinity."

hearts; when we first know Christ, being enabled to 'call him Lord by the Holy Ghost'; when we can testify, our conscience bearing us witness in the Holy Ghost, 'the life which I now live, I live by faith in the Son of God, who loved me, and gave himself for me.'"[10] As is the case with Christianity generally, so with Wesleyan theology: The dogma of the Trinity helps sustain a theo-logic concerning God's purposes and activities within the economy of salvation. Talk of the Son and the Spirit in accomplishing the works of God only makes sense in light of an intuited and nuanced Trinitarian sensibility.

Conclusion

Hopefully, the picture of Trinitarianism that is emerging is not definitional or explanatory but rather perspectival and grammatical. Christians came to construct the dogma of the Trinity as a way of making sense of basic claims surrounding their speech and worship. Trinitarianism is a working proposal, a mechanism of coherence that aims at a faithful account of what Christians wish to say about YHWH through the entryway that is Jesus, this first-century Jew who is proclaimed and worshiped by Christians as Savior and Lord.

Questions for Consideration

1. What is the basic problem with the modern privileging of generalizability? How does such privileging lead to a kind of violence against religious commitments?

10. "Spiritual Worship," 96.

2. What are the two layers of particularity to the church's confession? How are these two layers related and yet distinct?

3. What are the two instantiating claims of Trinitarianism and how do these claims make sense of who God is? In other words, how are Jewish monotheism and the worship and identity of Jesus related? Why is it important to ground the church's confession of the Trinity in the history of Israel? And yet, why is the whole life and destiny of Jesus central to the development of Trinitarian doctrine?

4. Share how John Wesley's work on the Trinity speaks to the importance of the Trinity in the Christian life. How is the logic of the Trinity incorporated into Wesley's approach to knowing God and to walking as Jesus walked?

5. How does the doctrine of the Trinity aim at a faithful, coherent account of the ways Christians speak of and about God? Why is coherence important?

three

Is Trinitarianism Biblical?

The last chapter claimed that Trinitarianism was the church's attempt to make sense of two basic but apparently competing notions: 1) the preeminence of YHWH as the one true God, and 2) the church's claims and practices surrounding Jesus. Whereas the first consideration is historically prior to the second, for Christians the second is theologically privileged over the first. In other words, Jesus provides the "lens" or the "grid" by which we see and make sense of God's being and purposes. This privileging of Jesus is warranted because through this One, salvation has come to the world. He was faithful until the end and in fact conquered absurdity and death for us, thereby marking a significant turning point in history. Christians will want to say that the Christ-event is one that orients and shapes all of history.

As important as Jesus is to a Christian self-understanding, some people have labeled Trinitarianism as unbiblical, and they do so for a host of reasons. One frequent charge is that the word *trinity* is not in the Bible, and its absence is taken to suggest that the idea is theologically irrelevant and so inapplicable to faith. Truth be told, the term is not in the Bible: *Trinity* is most closely related to the Latin term *trinitas*, and the word was first coined by the African theologian Tertullian (ca. 160–ca. 240).[1] The father of Latin theology was quite influential in shaping early Trinitarian theology, for not only was he the first to use the word *trinity* in formal God-talk but he also raised to prominence the language of "personhood" and the phrase "one substance in three persons" for theological speech.[2] These developments occurred in light of triadic forms of prayers, doxologies, and pre-creedal materials that marked the Christian tradition from the very beginning.

If the term *trinity* is not in the Bible, then is the concept present? Some passages do make allusion to the triune persons of Father, Son, and Holy Spirit as a proximate set, and these precedents make the use of Trinitarian language viable.[3] Detractors, however, can also point out that the relevant biblical passages are sparse and often plagued by specific challenges; therefore, some of these instances should be considered extensively.[4]

1. Tertullian represents the first Latin use of the term. Certain Greek writers (Theophilus and Theodotus) predated Tertullian in using the language of "triad"; see Prestige, *God in Patristic Thought*, 93. One should also note that triadic formulas did not indicate at this stage formal Trinitarian reflection; the pattern was simply emerging at this early time period.

2. O'Collins, *Tripersonal God*, 105. For an early use of the term *trinitas* by Tertullian, see *Against Praxeas*, VIII. Although space prohibits a more formal inclusion in the next chapter, Tertullian's influence on Trinitarianism should not be downplayed.

3. Essentially, this is the Wesleyan approach to reservations regarding Trinitarian language; see Wesley, "On the Trinity," 378.

4. Wesley did not shy away from such challenges and even en-

alluded but didn't say — actual words

The most prominent example of Trinitarianism within the Bible is the passage oftentimes referenced as "The Great Commission." Jesus instructs his disciples in the following way: "Go therefore and make disciples of all nations, baptizing them in the name of the Father and of the Son and of the Holy Spirit" (Matt 28:19). This verse is perhaps the most important Trinitarian example in the Bible because not only does it conveniently tie all three persons of the Trinity together but it does so with reference to the communal practice of water baptism, that sacrament of the church used to initiate new members into the fold. Consequently, the Trinity functions here as the name or authority by which new believers are brought into Christian fellowship.[5] In light of this passage, the vast majority of the world's Christians who have been baptized in water have been so in the name and under the authority of the Father, Son, and Holy Ghost. This pattern occasions the interweaving of confession *and* practice, something that the church has always considered important as it has moved to identify itself and to speak theologically. Nevertheless, the passage's authenticity has been questioned on textual, literary, and historical grounds.[6] These kinds of probings are important, but such forms of questioning do not take away from the manner in which this portion of Scripture has functioned for countless generations to secure a Christian understanding of

---

gaged in biblical textual criticism in light of certain cases; see once again, "On the Trinity," 378–79.

5. The appropriation of the triune names in relation to Christian baptism was quite early; see for instance *Didache*, VII.

6. See Wainwright, *Trinity in the New Testament*, 238–41.

the Godhead from the very beginning of one's Christian journey.

Other passages share both this promise and challenge. Take, for example, 2 Corinthians 13:13, "The grace of the Lord Jesus Christ, the love of God, and the communion of the Holy Spirit be with all of you." The difficulty with this passage is the referent of "God." Does "God" here refer to the "Father," the God Jesus claimed as his "Abba, Father"? One could make this move due to the thrust of other biblical passages, including Ephesians 4:4–6, "There is one body and one Spirit, just as you were called to the one hope of your calling, one Lord, one faith, one baptism, one God and Father of all, who is above all and through all and in all." In this portion of Scripture, "God" and "Father" are tied (as they often are throughout Christian antiquity), so the possibility inherent to the 2 Corinthians passage is scripturally justifiable. Nevertheless, a difficulty exists with this Ephesians passage as well, and this challenge relates to the term *spirit*: Whether to capitalize *spirit* is often a judgment call made by biblical translators, because the word is used both for divine ("the Holy Spirit") and human referents (for instance, "the spirit of Elijah"). As a consequence, some wonder if the spirit mentioned in this passage is in fact the Holy Spirit.

Many other passages could be cited,[7] but the difficulty still stands: The New Testament does not demonstrate

7. Other examples include Rom 14:17–18; 15:16, 30; 1 Cor 12:4–6; 2 Cor 1:21–22; 3:3; Gal 3:11–14; 4:6; Eph 2:18, 20–22 (with attention to the Greek text here); 3:14–17; Phil 3:3; Col 1:6–8; 2 Thess 2:13–14; Titus 3:4–6; Heb 10:29; 1 Pet 1:2; and Jude 20–21. See Wainwright, *Trinity in the New Testament*, chapter 13 for an analysis of the many possibilities.

a fully developed or consistently present Trinitarianism in terms of its outright, explicit claims. The triadic formula is not always present in ways that are consistent and compelling, and when it is available, either explicitly or implicitly, this presentation still does not betray a Trinitarian logic per se, one that accounts for the many complexities of the scriptural witness. Nevertheless, Trinitarian patterns are present in Scripture, thereby providing the groundwork for the Trinitarian theology that was later to be developed.

A "Primitive" Trinitarianism

These Trinitarian patterns in Scripture suggest something that could be termed a *primitive Trinitarianism* in the biblical witness. What is meant by "primitive" in this case is underdeveloped or not fully consistent. This reality has already been considered in a number of forms: the way that "God" may sometimes be used conveniently as a synonym for "Father" and the difficulty of specifying the referent of "spirit."

But perhaps the most persistent challenge to Trinitarianism has been the many biblical instances that mark continuity and discontinuity between Jesus and his Father. Obviously, discontinuities should abound: After all, in Jesus one does not have naked divinity but a human being whom Christians consider "God in the flesh." If one emphasizes the fleshly aspect of this holy mystery, plenty of biblical examples point to the marked contrast between God and Jesus. These passages would include the time when Jesus says that no one knows the hour of final judgment except for the Father (Matt 24:36; Mark 13:32), the prayer at Gethsemane in which Jesus prays not his will but the Father's will be done (Luke 22:42), the cry of dereliction in which Jesus claims to be forsaken by God (Matt 27:46; Mark 15:34), and so forth. Just the language of "Father" and "Son" already hints at a distinction between the two that could lead to the preeminence of the former and the possible inferiority of the latter.

"Low" and "High" Christologies

What to make of these passages and terms? In a broad sense, one could say that in the gospels a *functional subordinationism* does exist between the Father and Jesus, one that pivots on the reality of the Son's incarnate self-presentation.[8] The claim "God in the flesh" requires due recognition of the reality of human contingencies and particularities. The overall perspective that privileges Jesus' humanity (a stance some would characterize as a "low Christology") has in its purview these biblical instances in which there is a marked contrast between Jesus and his Father. These distinctions and contrasts make sense because of the infinite expanse that exists between Creator and creation, God and humanity.

Exceedingly remarkable, however, is the way that Jesus and God are also intricately related in the gospel portrayals and the apostolic testimony. In the gospels themselves, Jesus speaks with authority (Matt 7:29),

8. I should add that the functional subordinationism being spoken of here is not eternal because it operates under the revelatory conditions of the incarnation. I am grateful to my student Emily Johnson, who raised the need for this clarification because of the debates involving the Trinity and gender roles.

forgives sins (Mark 2:5), performs miracles, casts out demons, and undertakes a number of actions that show him as filled with the Spirit of God; in other words, he engages in activities often associated with divine functions. But not only does he claim Israel's God as his "Father"; he also expresses an intimate tie between this One and himself. For instance, the Johannine claims that Jesus and the Father are one (John 10:30), that when one knows Jesus one will know the Father (John 14:7), and that they coinhere[9] or are present in one another (John 14:11) all suggest that Jesus is not simply another human being or even an exceptional prophet. The angle at play here is that a filial and relational uniqueness exists between Jesus and God, one highlighted by the author of Hebrews: "He is the reflection of God's glory and the exact imprint of God's very being" (Heb 1:3). These many verses establish a view sometimes called a "high Christology." These instances coupled with the apostolic testimony and the church's early liturgical practices and speech patterns create the kind of conditions alluded to earlier in Chapter 2. Simply put, the worship of Jesus and the confession of his lordship both assume a "high Christology."

Which angle, the "low" or "high," is more important? As in so many cases within Christian theology, this either-or portrayal is less faithful than one that would allow for both-and. Christians want to say that Jesus Christ displays both what an authentic, compelling, and thriving human life can be as well as what the divine character looks like when victoriously confronting anti-God forces and establishing the peaceable kingdom. In other

9. As the term is being used here, *coinhere* means to be related in a nonidentical but nevertheless inseparable way.

words, both angles, the "low" and the "high," are useful for elaborating different themes and concerns. A "low Christology" proves vitally important when Christians are in need of identifying with Jesus and of having him relate to the variability and complexity that comes with human existence. A "high Christology" proves equally valuable in that it points to how the Christian hope is in One who is greater than any set of circumstances. The significance of Scripture's testimony is that it allows for both angles in a way that helps preserve a healthy dynamic between continuity and discontinuity in the divine-human interface, one that is graciously and beautifully bridged in the incarnate life of the Son.

Pressing Further into "High Christology"

Without losing sight of the importance and contribution of a "low Christology," one nevertheless is tempted to press further into the implications of a "high Christology." If Jesus really is God in the flesh, then one can only assume that God took on human flesh at some point in history. The movement is from God to humanity since God created and continually sustains humanity. The alternative claim, that Jesus became God, has been vociferously denounced by the church since such a move would blur the Creator-creation distinction, thereby divinizing humanity as a result. If the church's logic holds, then something of the Son's preexistence to the incarnation is assumed. A "high Christology" requires that God, including the Son, be beyond the limits of human contingency.

Of course, through such reasoning one begins to move into the abstract and speculative side of theology, but interestingly enough, the New Testament writers do not hesitate to pursue this line of thought. An astonishing exemplification of this possibility is on display in the opening verses of the Gospel of John. Not only does the Beloved Disciple go so far as to tie his gospel to the origins language of Genesis ("In the beginning"), but he develops both a distinction and a gesture toward coinherence between God and God's Word: "The Word was with God, and the Word was God" (John 1:1). This "Word" was "in the beginning with God" (1:2), and "all things came into being through him" (1:3). But more remarkable still is that this "Word became flesh and lived among us, and we have seen his glory, the glory as of a father's only son, full of grace and truth" (1:14).

Wesley himself picks up this logic when commenting on this portion of Scripture: "Accordingly the inspired writers give him [the Son of God] all the titles of the most high God. They call him over and over by the incommunicable name, Jehova, never given to any creature. They ascribe to him all the attributes and all the works of God. So that we need not scruple to pronounce him God of God, Light of Light, very God of very God: in glory equal with the Father, in majesty coeternal."[10]

Historians are quick to point out that the Gospel of John is most likely the latest of the canonical gospels, a theory that perhaps makes this "high Christology" something of a later development. However, if one analyzes the earliest Christian documents, which would include the

10. "Spiritual Worship," 90–91; note the echo of Nicaea here.

Pauline correspondence, similar claims are made there. Take, for instance, the claim of Paul in 1 Corinthians 8:6, "Yet for us there is one God, the Father, from whom are all things and for whom we exist, and one Lord, Jesus Christ, through whom are all things and through whom we exist." A similar logic to John's Gospel is present in this document that predates the Fourth Gospel by possibly several decades. One sees further traces of this line of thinking in what could have been pre-existent hymnic materials cited by Paul both in Philippians 2:5–11 as well as Colossians 1:15–20. In both cases, Jesus is not simply a human endowed with God's power but the one who was "in the form of God" who in turn "emptied himself" (Phil 2:6–7) as well as the One who was the "image of the invisible God" in whom "all things in heaven and on earth were created" (Col 1:15–16).

The witness of the apostles and the practice of the early church suggest that a "high Christology" was part of the fabric of early Christian thought.[11] The "binitarian" shape to early Christian God-talk was something uniquely inherent to early Christian literature and worship. As is the case with so many examples, the Apostle Paul could hold this tension by suggesting a continuity between Jewish monotheism ("for us there is one God") and an exaltation of Christ that is tied to his preexistence ("and one Lord, Jesus Christ, through whom are all things and through whom we exist"). Such patterns of speech

11. The point should be raised as well that Wesley found a "high Christology" to be at the heart of basic, nonnegotiable faith claims. Speaking of the distinguishing marks of Methodists, he affirms, "We believe Christ to be the Eternal Supreme God; and herein are we distinguished from the Socinians and Arians" ("Character of a Methodist," 34).

and thought naturally occasion further deliberation and clarification.

What about the Spirit?

[handwritten: Not talked about nearly as much]

So far the focus of this chapter generally has been on the biblical materials that highlight the relationship between the Son and the Father, and as such, this emphasis presents a binitarian shape to Christian God-talk. Nevertheless, this logic is in and of itself not truly Trinitarian since Trinitarianism would also have to include the oft-forgotten person of the Holy Spirit. This neglect of Spirit-talk is itself complicated by a number of factors.

The Spirit is not considered in the NT with the kind of frequency that Jesus Christ is. This observation, however, should not deter one from examining the fullness of Spirit-talk both in the Old and New Testaments. In terms of the Old Testament, language of the Spirit can be found in a number of places. For instance, just as God's Word is spoken so that all comes to be in the Genesis creation narrative, God's Spirit too is present, hovering over the waters (Gen 1:2). The Spirit of God is said to be in or to come upon a number of figures in the OT, including Joseph (Gen 41:38), Bezalel (Exod 31:3), the seventy elders that Moses gathered (Num 11:25), Jephthah (Judg 11:29), Samson (Judg 14:6,19), Saul (1 Sam 11:6), David (1 Sam 16:13), Azariah (2 Chron 15:1), Zechariah (2 Chron 24:20), and many others. This sample proves that the language of God's Spirit in the OT is quite widespread, and the language itself establishes multivalent understandings of God's self-presentation within Scripture.

In addition to this perduring witness of God's Spirit in the OT, one also has to consider the Spirit's role in the life of Jesus and the church. For instance, the Spirit plays a vital function in some of the most important moments of Christ's life, including Jesus' conception, baptism, temptation, and crucifixion. The Spirit is subsequently tied theologically to the resurrection by Paul (Rom 1:4 and 8:11), and Luke makes it a point to emphasize the Day of Pentecost in Acts as a moment in which people were filled with the Holy Spirit. These latter developments open up the question of "subsequence" in the NT as it relates to the Spirit. Whereas in the OT God's Spirit is sometimes portrayed as emerging from within the created order, in the NT the Spirit is frequently spoken of as coming, filling, or baptizing people. This last sensibility is cultivated early on in the NT with the preaching of John the Baptist (Matt 3:11; Mark 1:8; Luke 3:16), and it is sustained in the language Jesus uses concerning the Spirit's being sent by the Father and abiding with the disciples (John 14:16). This idea of subsequence is alluded to by Jesus as advantageous for the disciples: "Nevertheless I tell you the truth: it is to your advantage that I go away, for if I do not go away, the Advocate will not come to you; but if I go, I will send him to you" (John 16:7).

Whatever one wishes to make of the interrelationship of portrayals of the Spirit in the OT and NT, the pressures related to thinking of the Spirit in divine terms are significant just as they are for the Son. The point is registered through the language of the "Spirit of YHWH" found throughout the OT as well as the Johannine consideration of the Spirit as "another Advocate" who follows in the stead of Christ. Once the binitarian shape of Christian

God-talk was pursued by the early church, it was only natural that the discussion would move along similar lines to the presence and work of the Spirit. Wesley fully affirms this logic when he remarks, "I believe the infinite and eternal Spirit of God, equal with the Father and the Son, to be not only perfectly holy in Himself, but the immediate cause of all holiness in us."[12]

Conclusion

Interpreting the Bible in search of the proper way of speaking and characterizing God is a difficult task. Those who would skirt the challenge by saying that the Trinity is not biblical because the term is not in the Bible's pages have failed to take seriously the patterns of Scripture and what these would mean for Christian God-talk generally. The Bible does demonstrate a primitive Trinitarianism and a functional subordinationism, and on both scores, Trinitarianism is further complicated because of the nuance involved with such phrasing. Overall, though, the Christian church has tried to steer clear of extremes and to honor all the ways that the Father, Son, and Spirit are said to function and move within the economy of creation and healing. This endeavoring has involved the laborious and contested task of evaluation and interpretation across both time and space, and because its shape is so varied and important to Christian God-talk, the church's work on this score will be the topic of the following chapter.

12. "Letter to a Roman Catholic," 9.

Questions for Consideration

1. What Trinitarian patterns are there in the Bible? How do these patterns provide the groundwork for a more fully developed Trinitarian theology?

2. What is meant by "primitive Trinitarianism"? "Low" and "high" Christologies? "Functional subordinationism"? Are these terms helpful? If so, how do they serve to clarify the biblical witness with respect to the relationship between God and Jesus and the Spirit?

3. How is John Wesley's "high Christology" at the heart of Methodist affirmation and identity? Are Wesleyans today more or less likely to affirm a "high Christology"? Explain. What are the consequences of affirming a "low Christology" in the church's witness and mission?

4. What are the consequences of neglecting the person and work of the Holy Spirit within the Trinity, of failing to see the Spirit as divine? Is the Holy Spirit regarded more often than not as a "forgotten stepchild" in Trinitarian doctrine? Explain. May there be a kind of fear inside and outside the church associated with the Holy Spirit?

5. How may the doctrine of the Holy Trinity help us interpret and understand the Scriptures more faithfully and completely? May a strictly "biblical" approach to the Trinity inhibit our speech of God? Explain.

four

The Tradition of
Early Trinitarian Thought

The fourth century was a pivotal time for the church to clarify its thought and speech concerning the God of its communal confession and worship, and these developments led to what could be termed "the Nicene Faith." However, patterns were already at play prior to this century, and these in turn influenced the shape of Trinitarianism as it matured more fully. What follows is a brief survey of Trinitarian thought prior to and during the fourth century. These developments have proven to be generative and pivotal for all subsequent theological reflection on the Christian dogma of the Trinity. Implicated in such reflection would be Wesleyan and Methodist theology: As a renewal movement within the Church of England, Methodism generally upheld and promoted the great creeds of Christian antiquity, and Wesley generally followed suit, at least broadly speaking.[1] Essentially, then,

1. See Campbell, *John Wesley and Christian Antiquity*, 78–81. Wesley did eliminate the article that endorsed the Apostles', Nicene, and Athanasian Creeds for the American Methodist version of

those churches and traditions that hold to Trinitarian dogma broadly and to commitments associated with the Nicene Creed[2] particularly would find the work of this century important for the logic of their God-grammar. Although the figures, movements, and issues are all exceedingly complex (and incessantly debated within the academy), some major Trinitarian motifs and markers from antiquity will be considered in what follows.

Early Voices

Trinitarian reflection prior to the Council of Nicaea in 325 was similar to the form it took in the emerging New Testament: generally inconsistent, often implicit, and at times ambiguous. Although the Spirit on occasion was mentioned, the bulk of attention during this time period was directed to the elaboration of the relationship between the Father and the Son and their respective identities.

One prominent tendency during this time was the identification of the Father with the primordial act of creating. The Father was often depicted as "unbegotten"

the Articles of Religion, and Wesley from time to time did express reservations surrounding the Constantinian factors involved with fourth-century conciliar developments. These reservations, however, have not signaled for Wesleyan and Methodist interpreters a disposition on the part of Wesley to reject "the Nicene Faith" (see for instance Wainwright, "Methodism and the Apostolic Faith"). Therefore, it is proper to consider Trinitarian developments within the fourth century as part of an ecumenical heritage that those in the Pan-Methodist family can hold. That Methodist hymnals have adopted the Nicene Creed since the middle of the 1900s is further proof of this alignment (see Campbell, *Methodist Doctrine*, 44).

2. Usually, when the nomenclature of "the Nicene Creed" is mentioned in this work, the referent is to the Nicene-Constantinopolitan Creed of 381.

or "unoriginate" so as to emphasize God's transcendence. Once this gesture was made, the Son was said to function as the Father's reason, thoughts, or speech and as such was said to be "begotten" of the Father. Analogies (such as the sun and its rays, light from light, fire from fire) were readily employed by figures of this period to relate distinction and unity within the godhead. An important example here would be Justin Martyr (ca. 100–ca. 165). He argued for a Christian monotheism while simultaneously raising the point that the Son, as the Father's Word (or *logos*, the term found in the Johannine witness), was used instrumentally in the creation of the world. His view was that the Father creates *through* his Word.[3] This *logos* Christology was essentially "high," affirming that the Word and the Father are one before all things while both being involved in the act of creating. In fact, in apologetic fashion, Justin would go on to speak of how this *logos* was tied to the truth and wisdom present among pagans, essentially creating a bond between Christians and the wider culture.[4] The move made sense since Justin and others at this time were interested in showing the intellectual credibility of the faith to a broader culture that continued to retain its suspicions and extend persecutions upon the nascent church. Justin did on occasion use triadic formulas, but the long-lasting contribution he made to Trinitarianism was to retain a semblance of both

3. *Second Apology*, VI. At this point, Justin is betraying some tendencies that have their native home in Stoic and middle-Platonic sources. This strategy is one that has marked Christianity from its early beginnings: Philosophy and cultural-intellectual conventions have been readily used by Christians as means to adjudicate and resolve their internal tensions.

4. See ibid., X.

Jewish monotheism and Hellenistic metaphysics in his *logos* Christology.

Following the lead of Justin was Irenaeus of Lyons (ca. 130–ca. 200), a major church father who helped the early Christian church counter the snares of the family of heretical threats known as Gnosticism. Irenaeus too spoke of the procession of the Word in the work of creation. In one of his most famous remarks, he states,

> It was not angels, therefore, who made us, nor who formed us, neither had angels power to make an image of God, nor any one else, except the Word of the Lord, nor any Power remotely distant from the Father of all things. For God did not stand in need of these, in order to the accomplishing of what He had Himself determined with Himself beforehand should be done, as if He did not possess His own hands. For with Him were always present the Word and Wisdom, the Son and the Spirit, by whom and in whom, freely and spontaneously, He made all things.[5]

This quotation could be interpreted in any number of ways, but at play here is Irenaeus' concern to think of God as transcendent to the creation and yet intimately involved in it through the Father's "two hands."[6] As such,

5. *Against Heresies*, 4.20.1; see also the earlier remark in 1.22.1.

6. J. N. D. Kelly helpfully considers this theme: "This image, doubtless reminiscent of Job 10:8 and Psalm 119:73, was intended to bring out the indissoluble unity between the creative Father and the organs of His activity. It was the function of the Word to bring creatures into existence, and of the Spirit to order and adorn them" (*Early Christian Doctrines*, 106). Later, Kelly acknowledges that a dominant feature of second-century Trinitarianism is the image of the Father (as a clear gesture toward monotheism) and his internal intellectual and spiritual functions or his metaphorical hands (the latter marking

Irenaeus begins to speak triadically not so much in terms of doxological rhythms but in reference to salvation history: The Spirit guides us along to the Son who in turn leads us to the Father.[7] Essentially, God's Word became one of us in order that we could become God-like.[8] With this emphasis on the triune God's work within the creation, Irenaeus gave more attention to the work of the Spirit than his predecessors, equating the Spirit with the divine Wisdom of the OT and making the Spirit vital in the church's knowledge of God and its sanctification.[9]

One other figure will occupy us at this point prior to the Arian challenge. Origen of Alexandria (ca. 185–ca. 254) has been controversial for a number of his teachings, but he unmistakably contributed to pre-Nicene Trinitarian thought. He continued to elevate the Father as "unoriginate"[10] but moved on to describe the Son's coming forth from the Father through a process of eternal (and noncorporeal) generation. For instance, Origen remarks early in his famous work of dogmatics: "His generation is as eternal and everlasting as the brilliancy

diversity). As such, the model of persons and personhood was yet to come on the scene formally for Trinitarian reflection (see ibid., 108).

7. See particularly *Against Heresies*, 4.20.5. In an emerging pattern associated with the "Rule of Faith," Irenaeus speaks of the Father as linked with creation, the Son with salvation, and the Spirit with prophetic utterances (see also ibid., 1.10.1).

8. Ibid., 5, Preface. Part of this idea is tied to Irenaeus' emphasis upon recapitulation, the notion that Christ's life is a microcosm of salvation history effected properly and faithfully.

9. See Irenaeus, *On the Apostolic Preaching*, VI–VII.

10. This characterization of the Father creates a potential privileging, a kind of hierarchy which in turn can lead to subsequent difficulties associated with subordinationism. This issue is significant in Origen studies, and of course it becomes increasingly contested with the onset of the Arian controversy.

which is produced from the sun."[11] This idea of eternal generation proved very helpful in the Arian crisis. In conceptually securing this generation as eternal, Origen could make the subsequent move of labeling Father, Son, and Holy Spirit as three eternal persons or hypostases. In fact, Origen spawned a turn of phrase that was in direct contrast to Arianism later, namely the notion that "there was not [a time] when [the Son] was not." Origen elaborates the claim in the following way: "Now this expression which we employ—'that there never was a time when He did not exist'—is to be understood with an allowance. For these very words 'when' or 'never' have a meaning that relates to time, whereas the statements regarding Father, Son, and Holy Spirit are to be understood as transcending all time, all ages, and all eternity."[12] This emphasis on eternal distinctions helped curb to some degree the subordinationist tendencies detected by some to be inherent to Origen's Trinitarian thought.

Arianism

Trinitarianism reached a crisis with the development that would become Arianism. Arius (ca. 260/280–336) was a presbyter and popular preacher in the Egyptian city of Alexandria, and he (like many of his predecessors, as we have noted) valued the oneness or unity of God, which led him to affirm a kind of subordinationism over and against the Origenist teachings of his bishop, Alexander. What apparently marked Arius' form of subordinationism from other kinds was his unrelenting pursuit of God's

11. *On First Principles*, 1.2.4.
12. Ibid., 4.28.

unique and transcendent being. Apparently in Arius' mind, if God is truly unoriginate and unique, then the divine nature cannot be shared or communicated. The language of generation, for instance, even if marked by the qualifier of "eternal,"[13] suggests a kind of corporeal or physical characterization of the divine essence, and this move is precisely what Arius and his followers could not allow because of its close associations with the creaturely realm. Unlike modalists of varying stripes (who simply saw Father, Son, and Holy Spirit as interchangeable forms of the divine self-presentation), Arius saw a nonnegotiable and thoroughly irresolvable differentiation between the Father and the Son, one that led to a motto associated with the Arian cause (and one directly opposed to Origen's thought): "there was [a time] when [the Son] was not."

It would be very easy to depict Arius' concerns as strictly conceptual or intellectual, but they were also very much hermeneutical and so tied to the interpretation of biblical texts.[14] In this study, we have already noted the passages of Scripture that emphasize both a Christology "from above" and "from below." Arius had the tendency to emphasize the "from below" angle, suggesting that Christ could not be fully God since he did not know things the Father did, had a different will from the Father's, and so on. In this sense, the Son was "subordinate" to the Father. Maybe the Son was the agent of creation and maybe this

13. Alexander tried to maintain a mediating position within Origenist possibilities, stating that only the Father is unoriginate and yet both the Father and the Son are eternal. For Arius, this particular distinction could not be sustained without reversion to an affirmation of two self-existent principles.

14. For a brief survey, see Kelly, *Early Christian Doctrines*, 230.

one was created before all things, yet Arius decisively could not affirm the Son as God in the true (and not simply titular) sense.

Arianism, as with all heresies, never completely died. If one approaches heresies not so much as "errors" per se but "truths taken to untenable extremes," then one can see how they continue to hold ongoing relevance. Arianism accounted for certain features of Christian God-talk quite well, including the radical transcendence of God to the creaturely realm as well as those scriptural passages and themes that are usually associated with a "low Christology." In the modern period in which mystery and miracle were increasingly becoming less available to a secularizing culture at large, a form of Arianism became an increasing threat. In fact, Wesley made it a point to counter positions and figures whom he deemed as Arian or Socinian (that is, Deist) during his lifetime.[15]

The Council of Nicaea and Athanasius

The Arian controversy was such a threat to Christian unity that it occasioned the first ecumenical council. The word *ecumenical* has etymological ties to the Greek word for "household," and so an ecumenical discussion is properly an "in-house affair." A dialogue between Buddhists and Christians would not be ecumenical but an interfaith exchange; a conversation between Baptists and Presbyterians, however, would be ecumenical since both groups are within the "household" of Christianity. Crises

15. See Campbell, "Pure, Unbounded Love," 89–90 (especially footnote 15) for a number of places within the Wesleyan corpus where these challenges were referenced and refuted.

throughout Christian history have occasioned meetings for the sake of building some kind of consensus and unity in light of pressing questions or rival teachings. The first meeting to be considered as such in the post-apostolic era is the one convened in the city of Nicaea in the summer of 325 and attended by approximately three hundred bishops. Emperor Constantine managed to attend the meeting as well; he viewed Christianity as a way of uniting his empire, so he wanted the Arian affair settled quickly.

Several claims came to the fore as the Council deliberated and eventually developed the first form of the Nicene Creed as a way of combatting Arianism. These would include affirmations of the Son's identity with God ("out of the substance of the Father, God from God, light from light, true God from true God") as well as claims that distinguish the Son from the Father without undertones of the Son being a creature ("begotten not made, of the same substance with the Father, through Whom all things came into being"). In particular, the language of "same essence" (*homoousios*) created a stir, one that persisted even after the Council had ended. Extreme characterizations were thrown around among warring factions following the Council, leading to decades of ongoing controversy about how best to describe and preserve the Son's identity and nature in relation to the Father.

One of the great figures to support the Nicene cause during the turmoil following the Council was Athanasius (ca. 296–373). He himself was present at Nicaea, but he came to wield considerable influence only in the aftermath of the Council's deliberations. Ever the anti-Arian, Athanasius secured the Son's identity through a number of warrants, some of which have been considered throughout the course of this study. First, Athanasius appealed to the church's liturgical practices and materials, especially Holy Scripture, to show that the attributes of the Father are ones characteristic of the Son as well. Scripturally, both the Father and the Son are depicted in terms of wisdom, light, truth, righteousness, and so forth.[16] Another strategy for confirming the Son's divinity comes from the logic of salvation history. For Athanasius and other supporters of Nicaea, the agent of salvation had to be divine, for no one else besides God could do what was required to mend a broken world. A helpful opening remark from Athanasius' *On the Incarnation* suggests the tie between creation and salvation and that they are both properly works of God: "The renewal of the creation has been wrought by the Self-same Word Who made it in the beginning. There is thus no inconsistency between creation and salvation."[17] Elsewhere, Athanasius extends a similar logic to the Spirit: Since believers are made partakers of God through the Spirit, then the Spirit cannot simply be a creature. Quite the contrary, the Spirit also participates in God's very nature.[18]

16. See Athanasius, *Contra Gentes*, XLVI.

17. Athanasius, *On the Incarnation*, I. What appears as a remark depicting the Son as simply instrumental to the work of creation actually involves the requirement of God's nature. As Peter Leithart clarifies, "Athanasius argues that unless the Word is eternal and proper to the Father's essence, the Father cannot even be the Creator that Arians want him to be. . . . If God is to be inherently and properly a maker, he must have his framing Word, not as an external assistant or instrument, but as a word proper to him" (*Athanasius*, 72).

18. See *Letters to Serapion*, 1.24.

The Cappadocians

Part of the difficulty with how Nicene theology progressed right after the council was the way talk of the unity between the Son and the Father (often sustained through the language of "same substance") caused confusion. The difficulty was partly due to a number of words that often had a wide range of meaning both in Greek and Latin. The Nicene supporters who eventually helped settle this matter to some degree were the three church fathers often collectively referred to as the Cappadocians.

Cappadocia is a region in present-day Turkey, and when speaking of the Cappadocians, church historians often refer to two brothers, Basil of Caesarea (330–370) and Gregory of Nyssa (335–394), and their mutual acquaintance, Gregory of Nazianzus (329–390). The Cappadocians took the Nicene heritage and added further layers of sophistication that were needed at a time in which people were becoming confused over Trinitarian language. As such, their work helped establish some Trinitarian grammatical rules that have come to mark Christian Trinitarianism.

First of all, they maintained the Trinity as an indissoluble, interpersonal communion. Relationality marks the inner life of the Trinity so that properly speaking one person of the Trinity cannot be considered apart from the others since all three "coinhere" and mutually interpenetrate one another. Therefore in Christian worship, one could worship the Trinity through a number of formulas, including rendering praise 1) to the Father, with the Son, together with the Holy Spirit as well as 2) to the Father, through the Son, and in the Holy Spirit.[19]

A second grammatical rule, one depending on the first, would be this: All three triune persons are at work in the endeavoring that God undertakes within salvation history. In other words, when one is at work within the economy, all three are. In common speech practices, Christians often say that the act of creation is the Father's, the act of salvation is the Son's, and the act of sanctification or perfection is the Spirit's. At one level, this remark has a certain logic and rhythm of its own.[20] But a further adaptation of this sensibility would involve the claim that chronologically (or more controversially put, dispensationally) creation and the God of the OT (the Father) are tied, Jesus and salvation are joined in the gospels, and the age of the Spirit and the work of perfection are from the book of Acts forward. This way of thinking breaks up the divine unity and opens the door for modalism, tritheism, and any number of other theological errors. A Cappadocian logic would hold that creation, salvation, sanctification, and the other acts of God within the economy are properly and thoroughly single works of the triune God.[21]

19. Basil argues for the propriety of both formulas in *On the Holy Spirit*.

20. This kind of reasoning is sometimes called the doctrine of appropriations.

21. The point is registered in Gregory of Nyssa, *On "Not Three Gods."*

The Council of Constantinople

After the work of Athanasius and the Cappadocians (among others), another council met, this time at Constantinople in 381. Other meetings had taken place in the years after Nicaea, but this particular meeting in Constantinople was eventually deemed ecumenical, in part because of its affirmation and expansion of the Nicene Creed. One particular modification was the expansion of the third article on the Spirit.[22] The Nicene-Constantinopolitan Creed claims that the Spirit is "the Lord and giver of Life, who proceeds from the Father,[23] who with the Father and the Son is worshiped and glorified, who spoke through the prophets." In addition to reaffirming the basic claims of Nicaea, Constantinople managed to move in a more explicitly Trinitarian direction in that the identity and work of the Spirit were officially pronounced within the Creed itself.

To conclude, the councils that met at Nicaea and Constantinople in the fourth century serve as two bookends of one long, heated, and spirited debate about what Christians thought proper and fitting to say and believe about the Christian God. Many figures, events, movements, and themes influenced this process, but by the end of the fourth century, a certain stability emerged regarding Christian Trinitarianism. Of course, debates and de-

22. For a helpful comparison between the two texts of these councils, see O'Collins, *The Tripersonal God*, chapter 6 (esp. 115).

23. In subsequent meetings in the West, the term *filioque* ("and the Son") was included here (so that the Spirit was said to proceed from the Father *and the Son*). This addition as well as a number of other factors contributed to the division between the Roman Catholic Church and the Eastern Orthodox Church in 1054.

velopments continued after 381, but a sense of collective achievement is often associated with the accomplishments of the first two ecumenical councils. For this reason, the fourth century continually is raised as an important one for Christian theology. Its many developments and nuances must be lived into today as a way of retrieving the logic and features of Christianity's God-grammar.

Questions for Consideration

1. How is the fourth century pivotal to the development of Trinitarian doctrine and to the way those within Wesleyan and Methodist traditions understand the Trinity? How may the Trinity help us focus on renewal in the church today?

2. Why was Arianism deemed a heresy? How did the Council of Nicaea and Athanasius address and combat Arianism? State the primary issue involved and the way the language of substance created a stir among the Council members. What was the answer Athanasius provided?

3. What two key insights did the Cappadocians bring to the development of Trinitarian doctrine? How are these insights important to the Christian life and ministry?

4. What significant contribution did the Council of Constantinople make to the doctrine of the Trinity and to the way the church understands who the Holy Spirit is?

5. How may Arianism and other forms of heresy still linger in the church today? Is the notion of heresy as a "truth taken to an untenable extreme" helpful, rather than simply seeing heresy as an "error" in how we speak of God? Explain. Can you think of contemporary examples?

five

Imagining and
Speaking the Trinity

What has been entertained so far in this small volume is speech related to the triune God of Christian confession and worship. Such speech, however, is a risky undertaking. God-talk is dangerous. Holy Scripture points to this risk at a pivotal point in the biblical narrative: "Since you saw no form when YHWH spoke to you at Horeb out of the fire, take care and watch yourselves closely, so that you do not act corruptly by making an idol for yourselves" (Deut 4:15–16). These verses, rendered by Moses to the children of Israel as they were about to enter the promised land, relate pivotal instructions for covenant faithfulness. As accessible as the God of the OT sometimes appears (in terms of speaking, working, and being present among people), these verses indicate that such revealedness nevertheless did not have a specific form; a cloud and a pillar of fire are observable but nevertheless intangible phenomena. These qualities show a pattern of God's self-presentation in Scripture:

Every moment of God's disclosure is accompanied by a clo-sure of some kind. Even Moses—the one who communed with YHWH on Sinai in such intimate of ways—had to remove his sandals out of reverence when YHWH first appeared to him (Exod 3:5). The dynamic was further sustained in Moses' case when he was not privy to God's face but only to God's backside because of the claim that anyone who would see God face to face would inevitably die (Exod 33:20–23).

If the maxim mentioned above is true, then why the closures? Are these simply instances of God showing God's power and might so people can be reminded that nothing can compare to how vast God is? Certainly, that line of argument is possible, but perhaps more genera-tive for the theological task are the closing words in the Deuteronomy passage quoted above: The people entering the promised land were warned not to act corruptly by making idols. Idolatry then is very much a problem re-lated to imagining and speaking about God.

When people think of idolatry today, usually the ref-erent is to statues that people worship, and the assumed problem with this practice is that it substitutes something created in the place of the One who ultimately creates. Of course, such a claim is legitimate and biblically war-ranted, but the problem of idolatry goes deeper still. It may be easy to pass judgment on Israel for its many lapses in covenant faithfulness, but the underlying issue is quite complex and profound. Why did the children of Israel struggle so much with idolatry, and what is at the heart of idolatry itself? From one lens, one could say that pressures existed for Israel to be like their neighbors, and since these other peoples were worshiping golden calves and Asherah poles, then Israel wanted to follow suit. But from another perspective, one could say that human beings are at their core created to be worshipers; they are inclined to value and so subsume themselves to something else. Some have found this feature of human existence deeply problematic and have believed that emancipation from this mentality is the only way to pursue a free and thriving life. But even those narratives of emancipation and enlightenment can become all-consuming of the self who promulgates and lives by them, for humans can worship not only material things but also ideas. This feature of human existence shows that humans have voids that they all too quickly try to fill with what they think will make them happy.[1] *Yes I totally agree*

Idolatry does involve putting something other than God in the place of God in one's mind and heart, but the matter is so much subtler today than it was in biblical times. Rather than calves and poles, idolatry today involves those larger features of our aspirations that our culture and its many worldviews put forth as worthy of pursuit. In our society, idolatry can involve pleasure, money, power, fame, and a host of other possibilities. When one's tastes, delights, worries, and thoughts persistently revolve around such things, it is worth asking if idolatry has become a problem. And one should note that idolatry does not just involve things that are outside of ourselves. What is outside of us influences who

---

1. Interestingly, the Wesleys emphasized this point on a number of occasions, referencing in some of these instances the opening lines of Augustine's *Confessions*: "Our hearts are restless until they find their rest in Thee." See "'Awake, Thou That Sleepest,'" 148, and "Sermon on the Mount, II," 497, for a couple of these instances.

we are, and who we are illuminates what we see and so want. In this regard, idolatry is not just the business of putting something in the place of God but it also relates to the danger of naming features of ourselves as divine. The technical term for this activity is *projection*. In common terms, it involves making God into a "mini-me" or (maybe more accurately) a "grandiose-me."

Taking a Second Look at *The Shack*

To get at this matter, one can recall a work of Christian fiction of recent memory that enjoyed quite a bit of commercial success. *The Shack* is a story of a family that has had to come to terms with a major tragedy, and the narrative of the plotline moves to portray the father figure, Mackenzie Allen Phillips (or simply "Mack"), as meeting the Trinity. Of course, this development is unusual on its own terms, but one detail that was especially controversial to readers was the way the author of the book, William Paul Young, went on to describe the three triune persons as Mack encountered them: the Father was a large African-American woman, the Son was a Middle Eastern male, and the Holy Spirit was a small Asian woman. Particularly, the portrayal of the Father was very difficult for some readers to accept, and the charge of scandal and perhaps even heresy was leveled at *The Shack* as a result.

But what is really happening in this particular depiction of the Trinity? Careful and theologically minded readers will note that the author's portrayal of the Trinity has a certain rationale and that this logic is explicitly worked out in the course of the book's development. The matter starts to take a specific theological form when the narrator in the story relates some of Mack's thoughts upon Mack's encounter with the Trinity: "Since there were three of them, maybe this was a Trinity sort of thing. But two women and a man and none of them white? Then again, *why had he naturally assumed that God would be white?*"[2] Eventually, what ensues in this part of the book is a conversation between Mack and "Papa" (the narrator continues to call the African-American woman "Papa" since this is the name Mack's wife regularly used for God).

Two layers of complexity introduce themselves in this dialogue between Mack and "Papa." The first level is the issue of gender. Mack had a difficult relationship with his own father, and this difficulty played a role in complicating Mack's use of the name "Papa" for God. Mack begins: "You must know calling you 'Papa' is a bit of a stretch for me." Papa replies, "But tell me, why do *you* think it's hard for you? Is it because it's too familiar for you, or maybe because I am showing myself as a woman, or mother?" And then the clincher rings true for Mack, for "Papa" presses: "Or maybe it's because of the failures of your *own* papa?"[3] These questions show the complexity surrounding the use of a term like "Papa" for God. This word, like all words, is not neutral. Not only is this notion complicated on its own terms (since attributing a particular human relationship and role to God—the One who is ultimate mystery—is risky in and of itself), but the move is also difficult because Mack has a history with the role of fatherhood generally. Interestingly, Mack' relationship

2. *The Shack,* 87 (emphasis added).

3. Ibid., 92.

to his earthly "papa" made it difficult for him to call God "Papa."

The second layer of complexity is race. Mack is Caucasian, and his conditioning and his tendency to project contribute to the expectation that God would be white as well. "Papa" is aware of this situation, and she helps clarify the matter to Mack, "To reveal myself to you as a very large, white grandfather figure with flowing beard, like Gandalf, would simply reinforce your religious stereotypes."[4] Mack's stereotypes are both socially conditioned by Mack's wider community and also taken up and projected by Mack himself. Just as we learn a language and in turn use it in certain ways, so we also do the same with images, metaphors, and visuals in our God-talk. Once confronted with an alternative God-visual, Mack came to an astonishing awareness: "He believed, in his head at least, that God was Spirit, neither male nor female, but in spite of that, he was embarrassed to admit to himself that all his visuals for God were very white and very male."[5]

What Mack tends to do—as we are all prone to do—is to project in God-talk, to make God into one's own image through one's speech patterns and expectations. This tendency is quite natural but at the same time very dangerous. It involves the risk alluded to in the Deuteronomy passage quoted above. "Papa" makes a point to Mack that is very hard for him and all believers to recognize and accept: "The problem is that many folks try to grasp some sense of who I am by taking the best version of themselves, projecting that to the nth degree, factoring in all

4. Ibid., 94.
5. Ibid.

the goodness they can perceive . . . and then calling *that* God. And while it may seem like a noble effort, the truth is that it falls pitifully short of who I really am."[6]

The Feuerbachian Critique

Projection in God-talk is universal. Everybody who speaks of God tends to do it one way or another, and this tendency has led many observers to find such language unsustainable. The person often associated with this disdain is Ludwig Feuerbach, a nineteenth-century German atheist. In his well-known work *The Essence of Christianity*, Feuerbach assumes that the god of theistic belief is unsustainable, and because of that reality, what people are really doing when they are speaking of divinity is talking of themselves. Theology unavoidably and unmistakably is at its core anthropology. One quote can illustrate the point: "For the qualities of God are nothing else than the essential qualities of man himself, and a particular man is what he is, has his existence, his reality, only in his particular conditions."[7]

Christians will obviously want to argue the point of God's existence over and against atheists, but they would be wise to take seriously Feuerbach's warnings as they relate to language and the possibility, in Christian terms, of *concept-based idolatry*. When people speak of God, they inevitably bring themselves to the venture, and their selves would include their experiences, speech-patterns, aversions, joys, and aspirations. Within this web of pos-

6. Ibid., 100 (emphasis in original).
7. *Essence of Christianity*, 19–20.

sibilities any number of outcomes could develop. As in the case of Mack, one image ("Papa") might be unsustainable because of prior experiences with the term, its instantiations, and its associations. On the other hand, another visual might be quite appealing (an old, white male who looks like Gandalf), but obviously growing too comfortable with such an image is problematic, too: If God "looks" too much like our prior conceptions, then we functionally determine God's very self in our own eyes, despite whatever rhetoric we use to suggest otherwise. Projectionist tendencies are inescapable to some degree, and denying them simply gives ammunition to skeptics who will charge that religion is obviously and simply a humanly contrived system for helping people cope with the hardships of life and for justifying their predetermined values and concerns. A god who looks like Gandalf is simply not credible on its own terms, yet many people persist with such a visual.

A way of driving the projectionist point home is through a barrage of examples. Take, for instance, one's visual of heaven. What do we often think of when we think of heaven? Usually, we think of a spacious place with mansions, pearly gates, and streets of gold. However much one wishes to cite Scripture for support of such a visual (for instance, John 14:2), the fact is that this picture looks very similar to the account of Western capitalistic success. When Westerners think of happiness and bliss, such a visual usually is framed in terms of material abundance; having "stuff" is usually equated with success in our society. Since we do not liberate ourselves entirely of our histories, loves, and aversions when we venture into theological speech and reasoning, do we really leave behind the prominent ideas of happiness and success when we contemplate and speculate about what heaven "must" be like? Oftentimes, other theological topics suffer the same fate, including sin, salvation, and—the most daunting of all—God's character.

Given these kinds of determinations that result from us being historical and contingent beings, we cannot entirely escape projectionist patterns in theological speech. Such an admission does not necessarily entail an unredeemable fatalism, but this recognition is a way of being honest with ourselves and others about what is involved in God-talk. All speech, all thought, and all action depend in part on our conditionedness. Denying this feature of our embedded existence is to forsake the truth of what it means to be human. The difficulty, of course, is that with God-talk people venture to speak of One who is the "Ancient of Days," the Alpha and Omega, the beginning and the end. For many, the audacity involved with conditioned human beings speaking of an unconditioned entity like God is too much to accommodate. On their grounds, it is simply absurd to think that theological speech could even take place because it would involve doing the impossible.

And in some sense, this view has considerable merit. From the human side of the matter, theological speech is absurd, impossible, and hopelessly projectionist. People often use God as a guarantor of their private aspirations, the highest form of their selves, the vindicator of all their actions and choices, and so forth. Just because one confesses the triune God or has had a conversion experience does not mean that projectionist tendencies are put to the side. Quite the contrary, these inclinations form a collective burden that Christians must bear daily. Projectionism has to be continually crucified in its negative forms and constantly placed under surveillance and care so as to promote salutary and truth-generating outcomes. Christians must "take care and watch themselves closely" so that their speech enables—rather than complicates—the faithful apprehension and worship of the triune God. Apart from such care, what comes "naturally" could easily devolve into something unfaithful and untrue. The goal within this mix of danger and possibility is the cultivation of a critical awareness of when taste and preference run perilously close to excess or neglect. Yes, God is merciful, but God is also just. God is sovereign but also moved to responsive compassion, loving but also jealous and wrathful.

Ways Out of the Cycle of Projection

What ultimately keeps Christians from endorsing Feuerbach all the way? If projection is inevitable, what makes and sustains theological speech as true? The only hope Christians have in this situation is the faith claim and conviction they hold that God has truly presented Godself as One to be known within the particular circumstances (language, history, and so on) of embedded human existence. In other words, God has made Godself available so that God can be known as an object of speech and thought. Only the Trinity's accessible self-revelation makes God-talk meaningful. The Christian narrative allows believers to say that God has a history with God's people and that God presents Godself uniquely and impressively in the person and work of Christ. Furthermore, Christians hold that God continues to be possibly known through the person, presence, and work of the Holy Spirit. Therefore, the kind of divine entity Christians confess and worship is One who is gloriously present within the bounds of human reasoning and experience.

Much of these concerns are at stake with one major motif running through Wesleyan theology, namely Christian assurance. One of Wesley's most oft-cited passages of Scripture is Romans 8:16, "It is that very Spirit bearing witness with our spirit that we are children of God." This verse is the starting point of two of Wesley's sermons, and in both he defines Christian assurance along these lines: "The testimony of the Spirit is an inward impression on the soul, whereby the Spirit of God directly 'witnesses to my spirit that I am a child of God.'"[8] Wesley continues: "That this 'testimony of the Spirit of God' must needs . . . be antecedent to the 'testimony of our own spirit' may appear from this single consideration: we must be holy of heart and holy of life before we can be conscious that we are so. . . . But we must love God before we can be holy at all. . . . Now we cannot love God till we know he loves us. . . . And we cannot know his pardoning love to us till his Spirit witnesses it to our spirit."[9] Wesley does not trouble himself to explain the manner of this self-presentation, the "how" of its operation so to speak, but his conviction, based on Scripture and experience, is that it does happen. The testimony or witness of

8. "Witness of the Spirit, I," 274. See also the slight variation in "Witness of the Spirit, II," 287.

9. "Witness of the Spirit, I," 274.

the Spirit is the Wesleyan way of speaking of the triune self-presentation within the economy of salvation history.

Once one recognizes that the triune God's self-presentation makes speech of God both true and meaningful, one nevertheless has to admit an additional point: A human side of this awareness and task also applies. After all, the directives to "take care" and "watch yourselves closely" imply that the integrity of theological speech requires some sort of human stewardship. In the context of this role is where Christians need to remember Feuerbach's ideas. Like Mack, all Christians have to allow God and others to push them to the brink of having 1) religious stereotypes exposed, 2) metaphors mixed for the sake of avoiding the perpetuation of bad linguistic and conceptual habits, and 3) embarrassing realizations fostered that show the severity with which projection is so embedded within God-talk generally.

The Difficulty of Trinitarian Language

When one considers Trinitarian language particularly, this side of the human task relates to the specific aspect of gender discussed above in relation to the fictional character of Mack. When Christians confess God as "Father, Son, Holy Spirit," they are using two words that are inherently gendered. Naturally and rightfully, people have found this language problematic because of the effects it can have on believers. These effects can take many forms, and they can render a plethora of unhappy consequences.

Speaking of God in male terms has the propensity to make God, both explicitly and implicitly, male. Many will say, "Of course, God is neither male nor female," yet they will continue to privilege male pronouns (he, his, him) for God on the basis that Jesus was a male and that he spoke of the God of Israel as his "Father." A disconnect can exist between "what we all know" and what is actually said, and many wonder (again, rightfully) how this disconnect may cultivate both privileging and neglect in other dimensions of life. One cannot help agreeing in some sense with the charge leveled by feminists that "if God is male, then the male is God,"[10] for these patterns have a way of granting credibility and spiritual legitimacy to a male-dominated landscape. For women (and men) who have suffered discrimination, abuse, and trauma at the hands of males, confessing God as "Father" and "Son" may not simply be non-inclusive but difficult, threatening, offensive, and maybe even downright impossible.

Given such difficulties, should Trinitarian language associated with the "Father" and "Son" be avoided or given up? Some have tried to advocate for this possibility through a number of strategies, but the abandonment of this language undercuts the role of both Scripture and tradition within the theological task. If such language is easily dispensed with because of gender concerns, then such concerns become the ultimate criteria for evaluating what is holy and profane. Sure, avoiding "Father" and "Son" helps with the patriarchal problems associated with such terms, but what does such a change give up as a result?

Two points will be registered here. First, the words *Father* and *Son* in Trinitarianism are not titles per se but

10. This aphorism is usually attributed to Mary Daly; see *Beyond God the Father*, 19.

71

names. With such an admission, the strategy to replace "Father, Son, Holy Spirit" thoroughly with functional titles such as "Creator, Redeemer, Sustainer" comes through as illogical and theologically deleterious.[11] A name is not equivalent to a title, office, or function, and making this move in Christian God-talk is to reduce Trinitarianism to Unitarianism. The difficulty involved with bypassing the Trinitarian names is that it destabilizes the particularity of the narratives that rendered such language intelligible and depersonalizes the Godhead as a result. Case in point: One needs the story of Jesus in order to understand how to use the language of "Father, Son, Holy Spirit." If the latter is dispensed with, then the former's role is severely limited, for Christians ultimately believe that one can know who God is and what God is like only at the feet of Jesus.

The second point involves the difficulty of gender's inherent binary character. "Male/female" and "man/woman" are couplets or dyads that divide and fracture the human experience. Strategies such as the replacement of male pronouns with female ones for God only feed into the binary of gender and its troublesome misconfigurations. What is most needed in this situation is a destabilization and transformation of binaries, and such prospects are present in the triune God's life and self-presentation. For instance, the incarnation involves the healing of the most primary binary of all, God and cosmos. Furthermore, the triune acts of incarnation, crucifixion,

11. Wesley himself believed that "the quaint device of styling them three offices rather than persons gives up the whole doctrine [of the Trinity]" ("Letter of August 3, 1771 to Jane Catherine March," 270).

and resurrection of this incarnate God allow for an amplification of Christ's body so that those who are baptized and so clothed with and in Christ can lead a life in which there is no longer "male and female" (Gal 3:26–28). This possibility is realized because of "God's third," the person of the Holy Spirit who is at work not only to expose and transcend binary thinking but also to transform and heal those who have been broken by it so that they can live into the promises, desires, and expectations surrounding God's life and kingdom.[12]

Conclusion

God-talk is a promising and yet risky endeavor. It can be invigorating or idolatrous. The only way that Christians believe their language for God can be true is through a cruciform, self-attentive, and worshipful gaze upon the God of Christian confession. Christians have to take care and watch themselves closely so that they do not become too comfortable with their God-talk since faith can quite easily morph into projection. If Christians blithely participate in projection, the gospel ceases to be the "good news" that transforms and gives life and is corrupted so as to become the "daily news" that oppresses and kills.

12. These remarks are indebted to the work of Sarah Coakley; see for instance her chapter "The Trinity and Gender Reconsidered."

Questions for Consideration

1. What are the central features of idolatry? How is idolatry related to the mental activity called projection? What is projection?

2. How are concept-based idolatry and projection related? How does the popular novel *The Shack* reveal the projectionist tendencies we all have at some level?

3. How does the Trinity point the way out of projectionist speech and mental patterns? In other words, how does the confession of the Trinity make God-talk meaningful?

4. How is the Wesleyan doctrine of assurance of the Christian life related to God's self-presentation as Trinity in the economy of salvation? How does Wesley understand the Spirit working in the human soul?

5. What are some of the problems associated with gendered speech of God? What problems arise if we dispense with gender language? What kinds of problems are created when the church replaces the language of "Father, Son, and Holy Spirit" with the titles "Creator, Redeemer, and Sustainer"? Explain.

6. How do the triune acts of incarnation, crucifixion, and resurrection break down the "binary" character of "male/female," etc.? What are implications for the way we share in ministry together and relate to others?

six

Theology and Economy

The particularity associated with the God of Christian confession cuts both ways: On the one hand, Christians proclaim a divine being who is accessible and relatable, and these possibilities are generally seen by Christians as good things. On the other, this entity can easily be cast and understood in excessively human terms. In the last chapter, we noted the difficulty with language associated with the Trinity, that such language can easily be projectionist and descriptive of human ideals and power arrangements rather than reflective of the shape of the triune God's self-presentation. Theologians and others note that God-talk is inherently analogous; its referent is not entirely encapsulated by the words that are used to describe it. For every description that is used in reference to God, the conviction of faith is that those words fall short of what God expansively is. Our lips are unclean and the words we use simply garments; under the horizon of infinity, they only go so far. Part of the claim that God is self-revealed mystery is that God is always more than what we say, know, or think at a given moment and place.

Words are not the only potential challenge inherent to the particularity of the triune God's self-presentation. History is also a concern, for God appears in the Bible within the particularities of historical conditionedness. YHWH is the God of the ancestors, of Abraham, Isaac, and Jacob. This One is the "Ancient of Days" who nevertheless communes and is active within the covenant fellowship established by this One with a particular people in particular times. The claim could be made that Israel's history is YHWH's history: Not only does Israel peregrinate in the desert but YHWH does so alongside them; since the two are tied together, their histories and futures seem inextricably mixed as well.

God's immediacy within history is helpful in some ways, especially when the issues of despair and fragility are being addressed; nevertheless, questions also arise concerning God's nature and identity in light of this conditionedness. Take, for example, the case of humans: Over time, humans change in significant ways. They can grow in their intelligence and maturity, but they can also grow increasingly angry and bitter as a result of their pain and experiences. History and its broader correlate of time suggest movement and change of a kind that is not always premeditated or anticipated. Context, influences, circumstances, and experiences overall have a way of shaping us, sometimes beyond our control. In many cases, our passions, convictions, and concerns are not chosen by us but we are chosen by them in the outworking of our lives. If in one sense they choose us, then they constitute us in deep and powerful ways. We usually find such conditionedness both problematic but also enlivening. Humans do not like to recognize that much of their lives are shaped by forces beyond their control (including the ultimate leveler, their inevitable death), yet people generally find attractive the language of serendipity and romanticism. We remark positively that we "fall" in love and "are moved" to compassion when we are confronted with people and circumstances. This tension and ambivalence between freedom and determination are part of the human experience; they are by-products of living over time.

But can the same be said about the triune God? Many people find it compelling to speak of God as if God is moved by the plight of suffering humanity and that God grieves over the situations of history. And these believers have a good resource to back such claims, namely, the Bible! Countless examples from the Bible speak of YHWH feeling emotions, of YHWH's mind being changed, of God responding both to the disobedience and prayers of particular people, and so on. In these responses on the part of God, one senses that what occurs is something unanticipated and unexpected within God's life. The dynamic can be related quite simply: People prayed, and the Trinity responded; people were disobedient, and God punished. Some theologians and philosophers (including a number within the Wesleyan and Methodist fold) have used these instances to justify metaphysical claims in which God and the cosmos are intricately tied and bound within a process of mutual influence and determination. Within a variety of these proposals, the cosmos is said to be influenced by God, and God is depicted as being influenced by the cosmos in a lasting and significant way. Within such arrangements, each is occasionally portrayed as needing the other in order to fully be. From this general outlook, God and the cosmos appear to be on a similar plane and trajectory, and the vibrancy of their interaction pivots on the intricate and embedded relationality between the two.

These proposals help invigorate the interactivity often portrayed in the Bible between God and world, but they nevertheless leave lingering questions open: What is the difference between God and the cosmos? Does God need the world in order to be God? Is an emphasis on God's intimate relationship with the world the only claim needed to offer Christian hope for the future? However one answers these queries, church tradition has repeatedly found it fitting to accent something about God's otherness to the world alongside God's intimacy with it. This focus on God's otherness would include a recognition of God's antecedence or prevenience to the world both ontologically and eternally. The running concern for such a qualification is that a God who is too embedded in historical processes cannot do anything about their shape and course. God needs to be One who is not simply in the world but outside of it, and both aspects, how God is intimately involved *in* yet transcendentally *beyond* the world, are indicators of the way God is *for* the world's healing and repair.

The Immanent and Economic Trinity

Within the history of theological reflection, a distinction came to be that has been alluded to already. This distinction relates to the way that God is beyond time and yet involved within it. The terms sometimes used here within theological reflection are *theologia* and *oikonomia*. The first term speaks of how the triune God is thoroughly distinct and transcendent to the world. Christians throughout the centuries have claimed that "in the beginning God was," and they often did so without any self-conscious need for justifying or explaining the assertion. *Theologia* is sometimes called "theology proper" because its topic is God and God alone in terms of the Trinity's internal life. Within Trinitarian theology particularly, this aspect of God has been called the "immanent Trinity," with the word *immanent* meaning "transcendent" or "enduring."[1] The second term, *oikonomia*, comes from the same root as the term *ecumenical* mentioned previously. *Oikonomia* implies the purposeful and salvific divine activity within created space and time through the work of the Father's two hands, the Son and the Spirit.[2] Theologians who have wished to speak of God's activity within the world have sometimes spoken of the "economic Trinity" to emphasize this self-presentational aspect of the divine life.

At play in these distinctions between an "immanent Trinity" and an "economic Trinity" are not two trinities but rather the great divide of history with all its contingencies and particularities. In this light, two points are worth registering: 1) God is beyond any limits inherent to created being, yet 2) God is also intimately related to and embedded within such limits for God's greater purposes. The tension largely pivots on the claim that God is a self-

1. Since the word *immanent* could cause confusion, some have opted to speak of the "transcendent Trinity" in order to emphasize the same point.

2. Given this imagery, it is not surprising that Irenaeus is often associated as a theologian of the *oikonomia*; for a treatment of this term and its relation to Irenaeus and other early figures, see LaCugna, *God for Us*, 24–30.

79

revealed mystery: God reveals Godself so that what we come to know is thoroughly true of God; nevertheless, God is also greater than our minds and selves can fathom. Truthful and faithful God-talk does not need to be comprehensive or encapsulating in order to be so.

What is fascinating with this distinction is that *logically* Christians will want to say that the "immanent Trinity" (as mystery) is conceptually broader than the "economic Trinity" (as revealed), yet *experientially* within salvation history, the "economic Trinity" is what is known, and from this self-presentation of the "economic Trinity" one moves to speculate about the "immanent Trinity." This last claim was raised late in the last century by a Roman Catholic theologian named Catherine Mowry LaCugna. She wanted to make sure that the dogma of the Trinity would not fall helplessly into abstraction (which can very easily happen with the deployment of technical Trinitarian language) but would remain at the heart of Christian worship and life. She rightly notes (as it has been claimed throughout this text) that Trinitarian dogma historically emerged and continually is vivified within the worship practices of the faithful. She states the thesis of her work from the very beginning: "The doctrine of the Trinity is ultimately a practical doctrine with radical consequences for Christian life."[3]

---

3. Ibid., 1. On the same page, LaCugna writes: "Trinitarian theology could be described as par excellence a theology of relationship, which explores the mysteries of love, relationship, personhood and communion within the framework of God's self-revelation in the person of Christ and the activity of the Spirit."

Rahner's Axiom

LaCugna's work in large measure depends on a prior theological voice. Karl Rahner, a theologian involved in the reform movement of the Roman Catholic Church in the 1960s known as Vatican II, wrote a very influential book on the Trinity. This volume proved helpful in revitalizing Trinitarianism in the twentieth century. One of the major claims he makes in the volume is that *the economic Trinity is the immanent Trinity and the immanent Trinity is the economic Trinity.*[4] Now, this axiom could be interpreted a number of ways, and some of those may not bring to the fore what Rahner and others wish to say with the axiom. As it will become clearer below, certainly a strict and unnuanced identity between the two was not intended by Rahner.

For one to say that "the economic Trinity is the immanent Trinity" is not necessarily to reduce the latter to the former. When Christians confess faith in the Father, Son, and Holy Spirit, they do so with the conviction that these names and patterns mark God's eternal life. The manner in which Christians come to know and experience the triune God is within the particularity of history and its embedded qualities, but whereas the God Christians experience is real and true, the conditions in which they experience the Trinity have to be recognized for what they are. The most pressing example continues to be Jesus. Within the economy, Christians confess that God has been on display in a man's life, Jesus of Nazareth, the one who came preaching in the power of the Spirit and performing the Father's will. The recognition of

4. See Rahner, *Trinity*, 22.

Jesus, however, does not mean that God in God's life is more characteristically male than female because of this particularity. In this regard, the "is" in the first part of the axiom should be taken as indicative of truthful and meaningful speech. What Christians experience of God is truthful and meaningful, and yet God is greater than the conditions in which humans experience God.

The other part of the axiom may also be difficult to interpret. What is suggested here is that the immanent Trinity forms the primordial basis for the economic Trinity. God does not need the world to be God, and God was "in the beginning" in a way that the world was not; therefore, when God presents Godself in the economy, it is an act that stems from God's freedom and love to make Godself genuinely and truly known. This divine prerogative to make Godself known provides the logic for God "sending" Godself and having a "mission" to the world. Such language is of course biblical: Jesus speaks of the Father sending him to do the Father's will (see John 5:36 and 20:21). Also, Jesus tells his disciples that he will ask the Father to send the Holy Spirit who will bring to their remembrance all that Jesus has told them (John 14:26). The point here is that the triune God of Christian confession freely and out of love relates to the world that this One has created.

The Doctrine of Creation

This series of reflections may seem to be speculative and highly irrelevant to practiced faith, but such premature conclusions ignore certain challenges associated with embodying the Christian ethos. Many Christians speak of Christianity as being a worldview. Such a characterization has its limits, but as a heuristic mechanism, worldview-thinking can help illuminate basic features of Christianity that are tied with the concerns we have been pursuing thus far. Specifically, worldview-thinking helps us place God and God's role in the economy of salvation within a specific trajectory, one in which the importance of *theologia* and *oikonomia* can come to the fore.

A worldview is a lens or perspective by which a people come to interpret the world. The term can be misused if it is too specific in the process of classifying particular claims, since all of us participate in multiple and varied worldviews through our travels, friendships, communities, and so forth. It is very difficult to say that a person operates out of a single worldview. But what the notion of worldviews does help one see is the way broad concerns and their trajectories traffic in the public square. Patterns of thought, feeling, and action are detectable as one applies a grid of meaning to them; this grid could be subsumed under the idea of a worldview.

Brian Walsh and Richard Middleton have developed a mechanism for thinking of worldviews, and it is consti-tuted by four basic questions: 1) Where are we? 2) Who are we? 3) What's the problem? 4) What's the remedy?[5] The first two questions relate to what we have been con-sidering thus far in this chapter. Question one is not so much geographical but ontological; it involves the nature and origins of the universe and what these would mean for purposeful living. Tied to this first question is an ad-

5. See Walsh and Middleton, *Transforming Vision*, 35. I have modified the questions and their order as they are found in this text.

ditional philosophical query that has perplexed Western thinkers for centuries, namely, Why is there something rather than nothing? Again, this first question is not strictly about cosmological origins and explanations, for it hints at concerns related to purposefulness and meaning. The second question inherent to the schema of Middleton and Walsh significantly depends on the first: The way the significance of the universe has been secured will inflect in some sense one's anthropological account. "Who are we?" implicates a bevy of additional questions, including: What is the significance of human existence? What is a good human life, and how can it be enacted over time?

Christianity functions for its adherents as a way of establishing meaning, and for this reason many have resorted to calling it a worldview. Of course, to be a Christian in the first century and to be a Christian in the fourth century are two similar and yet very different realities. The same is true in our age: No single essence or kernel of Christianity can be mined apart from the contexts in which Christianity is pursued, and this admission creates the possibilities for multiple Christianities and so in some sense multiple Christian worldviews. Nevertheless, something has to hold all this variety together, and part of that need can be undertaken through a God-grammar. So, in terms of the first question ("Where are we?"), a Christian response might be, "We are in the creation the triune God has created." And as for the second question, Christians would most likely respond, "We are creatures created in the image of the triune God."

Making Explicit a Wesleyan Assumption

Wesleyans and Methodists throughout the years have found it important to stress the continuity and confluence of God and the cosmos within history. Part of this trajectory no doubt relates to the way Methodism early on distinguished itself from certain Calvinist or Reformed understandings related to the fall, sin, human nature, and human potential. Rather than stressing a perduring distinction between a holy God and a profane creation after the fall, Wesleyans and Methodists have striven to emphasize a God of love and to depict a creation that is capacitated by God to work alongside God in post-fall conditions.

If this differentiation is to hold, then Wesleyan theology requires an account of the dogmatic and theological theme of creation so that the interactions between God and cosmos are not inordinately emphasized from either side of the covenant relationship. Without a vibrant account of creation, the interplay between God and cosmos would tend to extremes. For instance, if God's role is too emphasized, then there is no place for creation to thrive and live into its fullness and integrity as creation. Alternatively, if creation's role is inordinately cast, then God is portrayed as dependent upon and requiring participation from something that is not-God, thereby representing God as something less than what most would deem necessary for God to be God. Usually, both extremes are resisted by theological traditions and figures, even if some of these obviously tend to one or another side of the spectrum. The only way to resist extremes here is to settle from the outset what it means to say that God is a creator and that the Trinity brings a certain creation to be that in turn continues to be the object of God's concern, care, and delight.

Again, Wesleyans and Methodists have not emphasized sufficiently this tension, in part because of their theological heritage. Wesley was occupied with "new birth" and "new creation" themes in his sermons and other writings rather than one's "first birth" or "primordial creation" as a whole.[6] This perspective is in keeping with the Methodist focus on being a *renewal* movement within the Church of England. Nevertheless, at least implicitly, any account of "new creation" requires something operationally understood about "old creation." If God does not give up on creation, the reason is that the creation is God's and only God's. God continues to recognize a God-granted dignity to creation given its origins and ends, and this disposition says something not only about creation but more primordially and definitively about the divine character. *The Trinity wants us to be*, and this claim is rich for what it says about God's gratuity, hospitality, and love but also for what it can suggest for creation's purposes and potential within God's plans.[7]

In this sense, the Creator-creation interface, when depicted in Wesleyan terms, is not competitive. The Creator and the creation do not vie for the same kind of space. For this reason, to honor one need not take away from honoring the other. Giving glory to God is partly a result of seeing God at work within the creation. And

6. This point is emphasized in Colón-Emeric, *Wesley, Aquinas and Christian Perfection*.

7. I more fully explore the topic in my chapter "Unearthing That Which May Have Always Been."

when the creation responds to God or reflects God in some way, Wesleyans and Methodists are prone to claim that within God-permeated conditions the creation can work alongside the Trinity to accomplish divine purposes and to render praise and glory to God. Creation is good and can participate and extend goodness because God, its source, is good. These many facets of Methodist logic require an operational understanding of the Creator-creation relationship. Only through such a framing can creation (and this would include its many contingencies, particularities, and embeddedness, including history) be understood in all its sundry facets, including both its glorious dignity *and* dependency.

Conclusion

Christians worship the triune God, and as such, they behold an entity who is involved in history and yet who is not threatened or compromised because of it. Rather than a monad or distant god who would be tarnished by involving itself in the world's affairs, the Trinity is intimately related and in solidarity with the creation that God has created. At the same time, this involvement can be redemptive, and so divine, because this One is beyond the world's contingencies and fallen conditions. Trinitarian thought in Wesleyan framing allows for God to be God and the creation to be the creation while affirming at the same time their intimate relationship. The purposes and ends of that interaction are surveyed in the following chapter.

Questions for Consideration

1. What is the "immanent" Trinity? What is the "economic" Trinity? How are the two related?

2. How is the Trinity a practical doctrine? What does the Trinity mean with respect to the way the church worships and prays? What difference should it make?

3. How may the claims about the Trinity help us hold together the worldviews in which we may live and move? How may the notion of coherence help in making sense of our different contexts?

4. What does the Wesleyan focus on "new birth" and "new creation" say about the way God is involved in creation? That is, how do Methodists and Wesleyans seek to frame the relationship between Creator and creation and the ongoing activity of God in the world?

5. What does the claim "the Trinity wants us to be" suggest about the relationship between God and creation? How does it help us address primary issues relating to identity, mission, and purpose?

seven

Encountering and Being Transformed by the Trinitarian Mystery

Does God really matter for our lives? This may be an odd question to raise, but it is one worth asking once one takes a look at one's day-to-day rhythms and activities. After all, how important is belief in the Trinity for how we lead our daily existence? Does God make a difference for what we do, want, and value? These questions are not so strange to ask because our age is a demythologized one; mysteries are approached to be solved, not to be beheld in wonder. Explanation rather than awe is cherished, so proving God's existence may seem more appealing and valuable than contemplating and obeying the Trinity. After all, do we need God when we can occupy ourselves with culling our resources and applying our energies so as to manipulate much of ourselves and our surroundings? Secretly, we may even think that belief in God may be more relevant and necessary for the marginalized, poor, and ignorant than for those of us who are "blessed." People who are established, rich, and educated may not think that God "fits" into one's lifestyle the way God necessarily would for those who are less "privileged." Therefore, God represents much of an afterthought in our society and way of life—that is, of course, until things go terribly wrong.

This picture may be a bleak one, but it aims to be truthful. For those of us in the industrialized Western world, we have actively created and sustained a way of life in which we try to assert our independence and control over and against God and nature. In fact, that kind of disposition perhaps raises the stakes all the more when something terrible happens, thereby increasing the severity of the "why" question. Rarely do we raise the God-question when things are going well. When crises emerge, however, many people start getting "serious" with God. All of sudden at such moments, God becomes very relevant because the superficiality of our self-perpetuated fantasies about how life and the world are becomes glaringly apparent. If true, all these remarks suggest an inflated sense of self-absorption and selfishness. We often manipulate God to be the guarantor of what we want. God is morphed into the enabler of our dreams, the provider of our needs and desires, the entity who makes sure the "good guys and gals" win (and incidentally, these people happen to be us). When things do not meet our expectations, we face a cognitive rupture or a break in our self-made coherence mechanisms, and at such points, since God is the guarantor of what we want, God in turn becomes the natural scapegoat to blame for our plight.

we usually call on him when things are tough

Transformation as a Possibility?

But what if the matter were entirely different? What if as humans we are largely ignorant, powerless, and needy? What if we have a penchant to forget and ignore what is important in life? What if God is ultimately what we need more than anything else and without God we are totally lost, yet that realization is complicated by the sheer pressures of the society in which we live? These questions point in a specific direction. The vantage point is one which puts God at the center and us at the periphery, a move that is difficult for us to sustain because of the lives we lead and the values we cherish.

The sensed need and possibility for this orientational turnaround come to us in the form of the gospel and its promise of transformation. For Christians, the possibility of change is available because God has revealed Godself within history as the triune God. Because of Christ, Christians believe we can lead lives of peace and ultimate victory; because of the Spirit, we believe we can inhabit the truth and live out of the power from on high. Of course, all of this sounds very pious, and for some people such talk is vacuous and platitudinous. Ours is a jaded culture, one in which a book like *The Catcher in the Rye* and political scandals make us suspicious of those who are in power and those who claim to be different and who promise change. Our culture typically champions the claim that all people are at their core conflicted and selfish. Given the skepticism and experience of our time, it may be difficult for us to believe that transformation can take place, that people can change, and that things can be different. *that is hard*

But without the promise of transformation, Christianity loses its bearings quite quickly. The "good news" preached and embodied by Jesus becomes just another iteration of the "bad news" all around us. Without belief in the promise of the Spirit, we are orphaned and left to our sick and selfish selves. All of us have made mistakes, sinned, hurt people, and fallen short of the ideals we hold for ourselves. If there is no way forward, not simply in terms of being forgiven but also of being changed, then our fate is our plight.

One of the major contributions of the Wesleyan theological vision to the modern Christian understanding of the Christian life is that change *can* happen this side of heaven. People can be different because of the continual self-presentation and operation of the triune God. Rather than relegated to past events and persons, the work of the triune God is at play here and now in the lives of the faithful. In commenting on the new birth, Wesley remarks, "by [it] our inmost souls are changed, so that of sinners we become saints."[8] From this particular Christian vantage point, we can mature as believers to be more and more like Christ in the power offered by the Holy Spirit. God's activity and presence are thus present realities to consider; they are available to those who have eyes to see and ears to hear.

8. "The Great Privilege of Those that Are Born of God," 432. Wesley continues: "[Being 'born of God'] implies not barely the being baptized, or any outward change whatever; but a vast inward change; a change wrought in the soul by the operation of the Holy Ghost, a change in the whole manner of our existence; for from the moment we are 'born of God' we live in quite another manner than we did before; we are, as it were, in another world" (ibid.).

Spiritual Lethargy and Dissipated Selves

But what does it mean to "have eyes to see and ears to hear"? Who has these capacities and how are they realized? Often when the gospel writers use that phrase, it relates to a statement (and implicit critique) of the way God is approached and known. Jesus uses similar language to chide the disciples when he asks, "Do you still not perceive or understand? Are your hearts hardened? Do you have eyes, and fail to see? Do you have ears, and fail to hear?" (Mark 8:17–18). The example of the disciples in this passage relates to a broader issue within the gospels, namely, that there are those who apprehend Jesus' identity and those who do not. Startlingly, those who should understand and appreciate his identity often fail to do so: The religious leaders, the learned rabbis, and other privileged sorts often do not recognize Jesus as Messiah. Unlikely others, however, often do see Jesus as Savior and Lord; these include sometime tax collectors, former prostitutes, the sick and unclean, the elderly, and so on.

A heightened scenario of this skewed apprehension is marvelously depicted in Gerrit van Honthorst's painting *Christ before the High Priest* (ca. 1617). In this biblical scene, Jesus is brought before the high priest and tried. Despite many proven false witnesses, two come forward with the charge that Jesus had claimed to be able to destroy the temple and rebuild it in three days (Matt 26:60–61). The high priest asks for clarification, but Jesus remains silent. Finally, the high priest asks Jesus, "'I put you under oath before the living God, tell us if you are the Messiah [Christ], the Son of God'" (Matt 26:63). In Honthorst's painting, the chief priest is sitting down with his finger pointed upward and a book wide open before him while he looks up at Jesus in chains. The priest represents the height of religious and scholarly presumption, and the Messiah in chains represents the irony of ironies. The expression on Jesus' face in Honthorst's portrayal is difficult to gauge, but Luke's depiction of the scene is suggestive: "They said, 'If you are the Messiah [Christ], tell us.' He replied, 'If I tell you, you will not believe'" (Luke 22:67).

Contrast this scene with early figures in the Lukan narrative, Simeon and Anna. In the case of Simeon, he was a righteous and devout man upon whom the Holy Spirit rested (Luke 2:25). When Jesus' parents came to dedicate him in the Temple, Simeon went and took Jesus in his arms, praising God and saying, "'For my eyes have seen your salvation, which you have prepared in the presence of all peoples'" (Luke 2:30). Anna, a prophetess of great age, came at that same time and also recognized Jesus for who he was so that she "began to praise God and to speak about the child to all who were looking for the redemption of Jerusalem" (Luke 2:38).

In the context of these examples, what made the difference? Why is it that the high priest and those around him could not recognize Jesus, considering it blasphemy when Jesus did not deny his messiahship? And yet how is it that both Simeon and Anna recognize Jesus practically immediately? Small details in Luke's depiction of the early figures are illuminating: Luke speaks of the Holy Spirit as resting on, revealing, and guiding Simeon; he also depicts Anna as a prophetess and as one who "never left the temple but worshiped there with fasting and prayer night and day" (Luke 2:37).

Spiritual Senses and the New Birth

In an age in which little is held to be sacred and mysterious, it is hard to make a case for what appears to be a biblical assumption: The way things are includes both an empirical and spirituality reality. Both the chief priest and the accusers as well as Simeon and Anna saw the "empirical Jesus," but one set of people "saw" a blasphemer meriting punishment and another group "saw" the hope of Israel. The discrepancy can be attributable to nothing less than capacities and sensibilities that are heightened in one group that are not in the other.

Wesley spoke of a "natural" condition in which people were in a state of slumber and their eyes veiled so as not to see spiritual realities. This state breeds another condition, dissipation, which Wesley defined as the "art of forgetting God."[9] In this post-fall situation, people are not sensible to the promptings of God until a change is wrought internally, that is until they have faith.[10] As Wesley puts it of the person who has not yet been born of God, "God is continually calling to him from on high, but he heareth not; his ears are shut. . . . He seeth not the things of the Spirit of God, the eyes of his understanding being closed, and utter darkness covering his whole soul, surrounding him on every side."[11] Wesley's language is reflective of his times. He focuses on "senses" and "sensibilities" in part because during the eighteenth century

9. "Walking by Sight and Walking by Faith," 58.

10. For an elaboration of the theme of spiritual sensibility in terms of faith, see "An Earnest Appeal to Men of Reason and Religion," 45–48.

11. "The Great Privilege," 434.

empiricism was prominent in philosophy, particularly epistemology. Nevertheless, Wesley is also appropriating a motif within Christian culture, one steeped in biblical and theological materials.[12]

Wesley typifies that moment when a person is awakened as the "new birth." This act rests on the foundation of Christ's work, but it also and distinctly is executed and brought to fruition by the work of the Holy Spirit. Wesley is worth quoting extensively in this regard:

> But when he is born of God, born of the Spirit, how is the manner of his existence changed! His whole soul is now sensible of God . . . The Spirit or breath of God is immediately inspired, breathed into the new-born soul; and the same breath which comes from, returns to God. As it is continually received by faith, so it is continually rendered back by love, by prayer, and praise, and thanksgiving—love and praise and prayer being the breath of every soul which is truly born of God. And by this new kind of spiritual respiration, spiritual life is not only sustained but increased day by day, together with spiritual strength and motion and sensation; all the senses of the soul being now awake, and capable of "discerning" spiritual "good and evil."[13]

Wesley continues the sermon with ongoing reflections about what it means to see with understanding and to hear with ears now attuned to the voice of God. At another place, he remarks, "And now [the new-born believer]

---

12. For a survey, see Gavrilyuk and Coakley, *The Spiritual Senses.*
13. "The Great Privilege," 434–35.

may properly be said *to live*: God having quickened him by his Spirit, he is alive to God through Jesus Christ."[14]

As is typical of reflections of this kind, Wesley does not emphasize the "how" of the event as much as assert its possibility. What is available to the believer in this life is not simply a relational change, one of status, but a real change, one of condition or being.[15] And this real change is enacted by the triune God of Christian confession. The Spirit awakens and quickens the senses of a person so that she may live in the fullness of the image of Christ. This person is continually inspired, breathing, and exhaling the Spirit of God. In another passage worth quoting, Wesley reflects,

> [The life of God in the soul of a believer] immediately and necessarily implies the continual inspiration of God's Holy Spirit: God's breathing into the soul, and the soul's breathing back what it first receives from God; a continual action of God upon the soul, and re-action of the soul upon God; an unceasing presence of God, the loving, pardoning God, manifested to the heart, and perceived by faith; and an unceasing return of love, praise, and prayer, offering up all the thoughts of our hearts, all the words of our tongues, all the works of our hands, all our body, soul and spirit, to be an holy sacrifice, acceptable unto God in Christ Jesus.[16]

14. "The New Birth," 193.

15. This turn of phrase is found repeatedly throughout the Wesleyan corpus; see for instance "Justification by Faith," 187; "The Great Privilege," 431–32; "The Scripture Way of Salvation," 158; and "The New Birth," 187.

16. "The Great Privilege," 442.

The new birth and the image of Christ should not be seen strictly as static developments. They involve sustained attention, for "God does not continue to act upon the soul unless the soul re-acts upon God."[17] A dynamism is involved between triune God and dependent creature in which the purposes of God can become ongoing realities of mind, heart, and body. In this sense, God beckons of us everything that we can possibly give because God is the source and so end of all we have and are. We are to render to God all that is in our power to give. This steadfastness is required not simply out of obligation but also in light of the realities of living this life over time: The spiritual senses can slowly dull because of negligence and even antipathy from the human side of the interaction. What this picture amounts to is a vision of Christianity that is embedded within the dynamics of *living*, within time and space and in the midst of the many variables that confront us. To have the mind of Christ is to walk as he walked.

On the Way

And if such a person matures in her faith, what then? What is this kind of life moving toward? Wesley repeatedly states that this life comes from and is directed back to God. And as such, this life can be considered in terms of depth, growth, and development, not just physically and emotionally but also spiritually. For Wesley, spiritual maturity is as viable a consideration as is physical maturity. He contends, "A child is born of a woman in a moment,

17. Ibid.

or at least in a very short time. Afterward, he gradually and slowly grows till he attains the stature of a man. In like manner a child is born of God in a short time, if not in a moment. But it is by slow degrees that he afterward grows up to the measure of the full stature of Christ."[18] For Wesley, the new birth is only the beginning of a life of growing conformity to God, one that will extend for eternity. Within this eschatological horizon, believers are assured of the ongoing presence and work of the Spirit to help them be more and more Christ-like. Such is the way of holiness.

In this journey, Wesley made it a point to emphasize another theme, one associated with the idea of Christian perfection or entire sanctification. This move has proven to be difficult to understand and perpetuate both in Wesley's lifetime and among his spiritual progeny. Of Wesley's many teachings, the one that has continually been misunderstood and ill-represented has been his teaching on perfection.[19] Of course, just the language of "perfection" sounds disturbing to our sensibilities since in our "I'm okay, you're okay" culture we repeatedly promote the tag "nobody's perfect." In Wesley's mind, however, the terminology of perfection was justified because it was present in Scripture: English translations often render a species of Greek words with variants of the term *perfection*. Take, for example, the New Revised Standard

18. "The New Birth," 198.

19. During his lifetime, Wesley wrote a number of works to clarify his perspective. On some points, one detects development, but overall one can see real continuity, as one can note through a comparison of Wesley's later works with his early Oxford sermon titled "The Circumcision of the Heart." One piece that combines a number of expressions on the theme is *A Plain Account of Christian Perfection*.

Version: Even with its modifications and alterations to past translations, it still preserves this move on occasion, as seen in its translation of Matthew 5:48: "Be perfect, therefore, as your heavenly Father is perfect." Wesley's inclination was that if the term was in Scripture then it had to be actively used and appropriated for it "to do work" within the life of the faithful.[20] This instance was one of many in which Wesley was actively seeking to promote a scriptural Christianity.

Critics have registered a number of concerns over the years regarding Wesley's understanding on this point, and many of these are warranted given the typical ways people consider the idea of perfection. People have worried that Wesley's vision overlooked the real struggle of Christians living in a post-fall world. For many, the idea of perfection involves having no sin or no desire to sin, and such states are simply impossible in this life. Dangers of spiritual pride, works-righteousness, and disillusionment have also been registered. These are appropriate concerns if the idea of perfection is taken in the way that most understand it, but the ongoing question is whether in fact Wesley defined the term the way most people do. As a matter of fact, the general push of Wesley's works points in another direction.

Wesley's vision of perfection is one tied to spiritual maturity or saintliness. Of course, claims of maturity or saintliness, like those of perfection, are difficult to sustain,[21] but Wesley found it unfathomable to predeter-

20. See his opening remarks in "Christian Perfection," 99–100.

21. Wesley made it a point to resist claiming such terms even in his own case (with echoes on occasion to Phil 3:12), a move that shows the (rightful) difficulty of promoting labels.

mine prohibitively if someone could be perfect or mature in the Christian life. Why? Because part of Wesley's logic is that every command of God is a veiled promise.[22] If we are commanded to be perfect (as Jesus does at the end of Matthew 5), then the assumption of Holy Writ is that the commandment is possible to heed in this life. God would not command us to do something that we could not do through God's grace and in the life God has given us. Rather than assuming ahead of time what is possible in this life, Wesley presses his readers and hearers to go on to perfection.

What does Christian maturity or perfection look like? A first point to register is that it should not be appraised quantitatively but rather qualitatively. Occasionally, Wesley himself falls into a trap by suggesting that a mature Christian is moved in "every" action or in "every" thought toward God; he is also prone on occasion to use such terms as "entire" sanctification. Such language only becomes fodder for those critics who would find Wesley's proposals to be highly idealized. Maturity is not something to be measured as much as a quality to be on display in how one lives. *Yes I agree*

Second, the quality that shapes and drives the mature believer is the love of the triune God. A life marked by Christian perfection is one that heeds to the Great Love Commandments: "You shall love the Lord your God with all your heart, and with all your soul, and with all your mind, and with all your strength" and "You shall love your neighbor as yourself" (Mark 12:30–31). Again, Wesley's veiled promise logic works here: If Christ com-

22. This way of presenting the matter is available in many of the works of Albert C. Outler.

mands these dispositions, then they can be heeded and cultivated in this life. A perfect or mature Christian is marked, characterized, and moved by the love of God in such a way that the image of Christ and the fruit of the Spirit are on display for all to see. In this sense, perfection is dispositional and outward-focused; its basis and intelligibility rest on an outlook and form of engagement made possible by the Trinity. The direction of this love stretches out to God and neighbor because it is the same love characteristic of the Trinity's life and the Trinity's transformative activity in our own lives. With the promise of such transformation and love, the Trinity, it would seem, is central to everything we are and ever hope to be.

Questions for Consideration

1. What difference does the mystery of the Trinity make in our lives?

2. What are some of the societal forces at work that may make believing in the mystery and transforming power of the Trinity problematic?

3. What is one of the major contributions of Wesleyan theology to the wider vision of the Christian life? How is the Trinity understood within this life-changing context?

4. What is the role of the Holy Spirit in guiding and revealing who Jesus is?

5. What does Wesley consider the "natural" condition of humanity or the problem of "dissipation"? What is the role of the Holy Spirit in prompting persons to change

and move toward God, having the mind of Christ? Within the Wesleyan framework, what happens to the spiritual senses when the Spirit quickens or awakens them?

6. What are some of the misunderstandings of the Wesleyan teaching on perfection or holiness? How may the confession of the Trinity help us understand more fully what Christian maturity or perfection entails?

eight

Ordering a Heavenly Society

One of the critiques that Immanuel Kant leveled at belief in the Trinity was that such a belief was not practical. For Kant, the heart of religion was ethics. The main concern of religion, and so Christianity, ought to be what one does, rather than what ones believes.[1] He privileged actions because many of the beliefs associated with traditional theological themes could not be justified rationally or deliberatively since the notions in question exceeded the capacities of human knowing. In Kant's mind, such was the case with the Trinity. He averred: "The doctrine of the Trinity, taken literally, has *no practical relevance at all*, even if we think we understand it; and it is even more clearly irrelevant if we realize that it transcends all our concepts."[2] Kant did not wish to speculate for the sake of speculation; his concerns related to "life on

1. Put another way, Kant's view of faith is based on practical rather than theoretical reason.

2. "The Conflict of the Faculties," 264.

the ground," and the Christian dogma of the Trinity (at least for him) tends to sound more like speculation than something that matters for everyday life.

People have long held Kant's view. All the technical and sophisticated language (including eternal generation, eternal spiration, same essence, divine personhood, and so on) can be overwhelming, and the impatient observer could say at the end of the day, "So what? Does this all really matter?" Hopefully, throughout the course of this text, the reader has come to see part of the importance of Trinitarian dogma for Christian existence. At a basic level, Christian existence *depends on and is made possible by* the Trinity: a God who saves us must be a God who is both with us and beyond us. The entire logic of salvation history rests on a triune understanding of God. Christian worship is also involved here. Christians receive gifts and graces from the Trinity and they in turn render glory and thanksgiving back to God within a dynamism that is thoroughly Trinitarian.

However, another dimension of the Trinity's "practicality" is worth noting, and this particular feature has gained quite a following in recent years. This aspect is sometimes labeled "social Trinitarianism," and its main tenet is that *a working understanding of the Trinity's self-presentation provides humans with an imaginative, fruitful, and peaceful way of relating.* Of course, this claim is a bold and vast one, but it has the capacity to be generative, both critically and constructively, for a communal ethos that aspires to be a sign of the kingdom of God.

Order within the Trinity

As noted previously in this study, the early church moved toward Trinitarianism as a way of making sense of 1) the monotheism of the Old Testament/Judaism and 2) the beliefs and practices associated with the person and work of Jesus Christ. One prominent strategy was to equivocate between the term "God" and Jesus' "Father." This move helped preserve a general movement from the first to the second claim. In other words, the diversity implied by the language of the Son and the Spirit was subsumed under a broader monotheistic logic of God as Father. The language of "sending" and "mission" further reinforced this tendency. The general move was to speak of God's Word and God's Spirit, with the name "God" being interchangeable in some basic way with the person of the Father. This way of making sense of the two claims mentioned above represents an early Trinitarian logic.

This particular strategy can be called monarchian because it emphasizes "one source" or "one rule" within Trinitarian life.[3] Within this understanding, the Son is eternally generated from the Father and the Spirit eternally proceeds from the same. The pattern positions the Father as the source or "font" of divinity. One should note that monarchianism is not necessarily wrong, and the logic was so widespread in the early church that often teachers who were deemed both orthodox and hereti-

3. I am using the term *monarchianism* generically. It can have specific connotations related to adoptionism and modalism (and when it does, I believe it should be qualified), but I mean to use the term presently as a category that contains ways that God's inner life has been depicted so as to privilege the Father as the "one source" of the other triune persons.

cal by subsequent generations often shared monarchian sensibilities. Their differences were not so much based on the legitimacy of monarchianism as much as the degree and extent of this framing within particular Trinitarian proposals. For some, the sensibility was extended to such a degree that the Son and Spirit were necessarily depicted as made or constituted in a creaturely way (as we have noted, for instance, with Arianism).

Is monarchianism required for Trinitarianism to make sense? For many early figures, the answer would be yes. In their minds, a principle or ground was needed by which to secure the coherence of diversity. An ordering mechanism or an interpretive grid was crucial so that difference within the godhead would not irretrievably devolve to disorder, the latter represented in part through the option of tritheism. But interestingly, tritheism has never really been a serious threat in Christian reflection. Proposals overextending the oneness or unity of the godhead, however, have repeatedly proven to be difficult. Because of this history, monarchianism and monotheism have often gone hand in hand in Christian thought in varying forms.[4]

Very serious controversies have emerged regarding the inner-Trinitarian relations, the most pronounced of which relates to the term *filioque* and its addition to the Nicene Creed by a Western council in the sixth century, a move that proved to be decisive in the schism between the Roman Catholic Church and the Eastern Orthodox Church in 1054. Nevertheless in these sundry matters related to the inner-Trinitarian life, one cannot help but

4. At least, this is a running argument for many today, including Jürgen Moltmann; see *The Trinity and the Kingdom*, chapters 4 and 5.

recognize that the focus largely has been on *theologia* as distinguished from *oikonomia*. In truth (as noted earlier in this study), the two form an inseparable bond; one cannot manage to say something coherent about one aspect apart from the other. Admittedly, talk related to the inner-Trinitarian life and its many aspects has had a way of overshadowing the practice and embodiment of Christianity.

The Trinity as a Social Reality and Vision

For some of those who have managed to find monarchian strategies incompatible to Trinitarian thought patterns, the way to reconnect Trinitarianism and the economy is clear: To think of the Trinity as providing a "social program,"[5] that is, a model by which human relationships can thrive and function. What this move entails is a commitment to a unified diversity[6] in the triune God's self-presentation in history with the understanding that this vision is suggestive for human social life. Of course, this kind of reflection can easily devolve into the projection denounced earlier in this study,[7] especially if these con-

5. This turn of phrase is associated with Nicholas Fedorov; for an article that extends this impulse, see Volf, "'The Trinity Is Our Social Program.'" Volf prefers the language of "social vision" rather than "social program" (despite his article title), a move with which I concur.

6. Or as John of Damascus puts it, a threeness "united without confusion and divided without separation" (*Exposition of the Orthodox Faith*, 1.8).

7. A powerful critique of social Trinitarianism in terms of its projectionist dangers is Karen Kilby, "Perichoresis and Projection." The kinds of projection in this case can stem from a number of camps; as Catherine Mowry LaCugna notes, "These projections [of human

siderations go on to specify particular courses of action, concrete ways of political involvement, and so forth.[8] This risk, however, need not prohibit this kind of endeavoring, for after all, if the Trinity is inherently relational and if we are called to be like God in some ways (as implied by the perfection passage in Matthew 5:48), then God's relatedness can be said to be influential for how humans interact in their relationships. In fact, God's self-presentation within the economy could itself be indicative of a new social reality. In light of this intuition, some relevant motifs will be explored.

Power

Oftentimes the way humans interact with one another is through organizational schemes that have "top-down" approaches to decision-making and valuation. Take the example of CEOs: Not only do they have the ability to "hire and fire," but they also are the best-paid employees within corporations. Such arrangements suggest power schemes. In our conventional ways of speaking and thinking, power involves such matters as ability, capacity, influence, strength, and control. People "seek power" in order to wield influence, make decisions, attain honor, and shape outcomes. Only few can have such power and so many spend lifetimes trying to achieve it. Sometimes

---

values] can take the form of a hierarchically ordered *or* an egalitarian social arrangement. In both cases, what is usually missing is a firm basis in salvation history" ("God in Communion with Us," 91).

8. Volf notes the irony that people sometimes make competing or opposing claims based on the same Trinitarian foundation. See "'Trinity Is Our Social Program,'" 419–20 n. 14.

people seek power with the intent of ordering wrongs and showing benevolence; nevertheless, we also on occasion cite the phrase "absolute power corrupts absolutely." Because of the mixed way in which power can be used, some claim that it is amoral and that its use can be either for good or ill.

But what is a Trinitarian account of power? One way of pursuing an answer to this question is through various features of the Son's journey on this earth. The incarnation, for instance, indicates one of the triune persons taking on the weak and vulnerable conditions of fallen humanity. The fragility of such a state is evident for each of us to see, but the Son voluntarily took it up both freely and out of obedience to the Father and under the prompting of the Holy Spirit. That the Son did so was not simply to save us. The end result is not solely the all-important matter here but the *manner* in which God chooses to save us is significant as well because it suggests something of the divine character. In this case, the Trinity demonstrates God's power to save through human weakness, a kind of weakness that leads to its natural consequence, death. What these points help register is an account of divine power that is very different from what we typically associate with the term. Power, according to the triune self-presentation, involves obedience, servitude, and self-sacrifice. By beginning with the incarnate Son who comes from the Father and who is empowered by the Spirit, we can have our minds renewed as to what Christian power can and ought to look like.[9]

9. Kathryn Tanner hints at this possibility quite effectively: "If Jesus is Lord but, unlike human lords, he humbly serves others at dire cost to himself, that says something about the true character of

Mutuality

The divine life, for it to be characterized by diversity and unity, requires some account of mutuality. This theme is often secured through the Trinitarian term *perichoresis*. This word has Greek roots relating to the ideas of "circularity" and "dancing/movement." Popularized by John of Damascus,[10] perichoresis suggests that the inner triune life is a fellowship of movement, reciprocity, and mutual indwelling or coinherence. A prominent passage illustrating this point (and cited by the Damascene himself) comes from the words of Jesus as depicted in the Gospel of John: "I am in the Father and the Father is in me" (14:11).

Rather than a static being, the Trinity is vibrant and ever-moving so that actuality and potentiality are fully and simultaneously realized. Within this perichoretic dynamic, the activities of "receiving" and "giving" are only conceptually distinguishable because in God's very self they take place all at once. Exchange, self-donation, and reception of the other are features of the divine life. Again, one finds resonances of this dynamic within a scriptural logic. The work of the Spirit, for instance, brings to remembrance and actualizes the power of the deeds and words of the Son (John 14:26). The Spirit sanctifies all creation through a peregrination that seeks its end in the Father. With the work of the Spirit, as with the work of the Trinity as a whole, no single person or work is privileged over the other. Creation is a work of the triune God, as is

---

lordship and about why we should be disappointed with every human lord we know" ("Trinity," 320).

10. See *Exposition of the Orthodox Faith*, 1.8.

salvation, sanctification, and so forth. In the divine self-presentation within the economy, a "perfect giving-and-receiving" is at play so that control, rebellion, obstinacy, greed, and any other relational fault and vice are excluded from the way God works and is in relation to the cosmos. Scriptural Trinitarianism suggests synchronicity, balance, order, and vibrancy.

When just and free exchanges take place within human relationships so that the dignity and well-being of all participants involved are recognized, something akin or analogous to perichoresis is taking place at a human level. Of course, so many of our relationships are marked by something other than a "perfect giving-and-receiving," but those relationships that endure and that are life-giving are ones in which a mutual regard one for another is at play. The point here is to emphasize the quality, form, and character of our relating one to another, and those features can be highlighted and reimagined in light of what one sees in the triune God's self-presentation. Admittedly, the gap between divine and human persons is infinite, but given that God meets us in the economy, gleanings of the Trinitarian shape of interdependence, coinherence, and mutuality can be both cultivated and enacted within human interactions. Such correspondences are only possible because of God's hospitality, which involves both the invitation by God to befriend God and also the possibility to participate in a species of coinherence within the triune life itself.[11]

11. These claims are readily found in John's "Farewell Discourse" (John 14–17).

Covenant Faithfulness

As hinted to earlier, the divine attributes privileged in God-talk should be thoroughly Trinitarian and relational. For God to have a capacity or ability to do something says very little about the divine character; for God to act concretely and decisively in particular circumstances is illuminating, encouraging, and in some sense beckoning. Therefore, the "omni-" attributes[12] are not as helpful as ones related to God's mercy, righteousness, and compassion. The latter qualities are on display in God's covenant faithfulness in a way that the former are not. Christians do pursue this strategy to some degree with their tendency to privilege the relational quality of love in their God-talk, and this tendency can be fruitful if it is exposed to ongoing surveillance and scrutiny because of projectionist dangers associated with the language of love. One way of engaging in such a process of restraint is by recalling the covenant narrative, one in which God has placed Godself in ongoing relationship with God's people.

Part of this covenant narrative involves a bevy of attributes and qualities, including goodness. When paired with love, goodness can depict the divine character within a context of God's activity to repair and heal the world from its ills and faults. In this sense, "God so loved the world" takes on a different quality when one also emphasizes God's goodness. God loves because God is good; God is good and so God loves. Love and goodness can work in tandem as a way of restraining the dangers associated with sentimentalizing God's love, but this

12. These would include omnipotent (all-powerful), omniscient (all-knowing), and omnipresent (ever-present).

move also helps with the rationale behind God's work: God loves the world because not only is God good but the world God creates is good as well since it comes from God. And so, "God so loved the world" says something about God's goodness and in turn something about the cosmos' nature as well.

When moving to the human realm, Christian disciples are called to love God supremely and their neighbor as themselves. The disposition of God toward creation is what creation itself is called to embody and foster. Of course, this call is not easy, especially if one's neighbors happen to be one's enemies. The rationale for loving enemies is that God has loved and continues to love them since they are God's creatures. That Christ can ask the Father to forgive his enemies because they do not know what they do (Luke 23:34) is a sign and model of enemy-love. Christians pray for and even love their enemies, not because they approve of their actions but because Christ was enabled by the Spirit to love and die for his enemies. Enemy-love, then, is tied to the triune God's covenant faithfulness to the creation that God brought to be. God's patient lovingkindness, as displayed in Christ's work of long-suffering (which is a species of patience enabled by the Spirit and so available within the church today), represents a Trinitarian form of social engagement.

Social Holiness

Wesley is famous for the phrase "no holiness but social holiness."[13] Often, this quote is used to support the idea

---

13. "Preface to List of Poetical Works," 321.

that Christians broadly and those within the Methodist fold specifically are called to embody their faith through social action. Naturally, Christians are called to embody their commitments as they seek to participate in God's work of healing the world, but this application of this particular quote is wrong. What Wesley meant by social holiness in this context was the opposite of "solitary religion." In other words, Wesley's understanding of the Christian life was one that envisioned relationships as at the core of Christian vitality. For Wesley, to be disengaged with others hampers (rather than purifies) Christian existence.

This call to social holiness was evident in the many ways Wesley and his followers strove to organize their revivalist movement. This tendency was in keeping with Methodist origins. Rather than a strict revivalist movement, Methodism emerged in the context of young college students striving together in one another's company for growth in holiness.[14] Certainly, the movement came to exhibit qualities associated with evangelical revivals in the modern period, but one of the features that made Methodism distinct was its origins and ongoing perpetuation of different group and organizational settings. These structures included the society, the class meeting, and the bands.

Wesley understood that growth in the Christian life could not take place outside of communal arrangements. Part of this commitment stems from the way the Love Commandments are outward directed. But also, this view is informed by an implicit anthropology, one that sees humans as functioning at their best when they are

14. An elaborate consideration of this time period can be found in Heitzenrater, *Wesley and the People Called Methodists*, chapter 2.

challenged and supported by others. Creatures are created out of Trinitarian relationship for relationships with God and one another. That is why Wesley's varying organizational structures should not be seen as incidental but rather as essential to the realization of his understanding of Christian maturity or perfection.[15] Growing in conformity to the image of Christ and increasingly sensible to the promptings of the Holy Spirit requires a fellowship of disciples. Implicit in Wesley's denunciation of "solitary religion" is a working understanding of who God is and what God has created humans to be, namely beings who thrive and grow in relationships.

Conclusion

Kant was right to think that the Trinity was irrelevant when approached as a philosophical abstraction since at the end of the day such a construct has no relevance to life. But on this point, Kant's assumption about Trinitarianism is mistaken. The Christian dogma of the Trinity is misconstrued if it is understood as an abstraction that gets in the way of "real life." Quite the contrary, the Trinity makes Christian existence possible. Furthermore, a running depiction of Trinitarian relatedness can inspire the Christian imagination in terms of what relationships can be and look like today in light of the kingdom Jesus has ushered. The Trinity's self-presentation, whether it relates to a reconstrual of power or a reconfiguration of how one relates to enemies, can prompt our social imaginations

15. This impulse is further pursued in Castelo, "Perfecting One Another."

to envision different ways of being together. Our communal lives, then, and not simply our individual selves, can image God's triune self, all because God has made a particular kind of communal life possible, one that is starkly different from how we typically experience our social realities.

Questions for Consideration

1. How does Immanuel Kant's view of Trinitarian doctrine represent an ongoing challenge to understanding the practicality of the Trinity for Christian existence and social relations? That is, how does Kant's view represent a mistaken assumption of the Trinity? Explain. How is Kant's view still pertinent to discussion about the Trinity?

2. How may the notion of "social Trinitarianism" generate imaginative and fruitful ways of relating to one another? What dangers may projection play in the way we practice the Trinity in our relationships with others in community? How may the Trinity serve as a corrective to these projections?

3. What does the "manner" in which God saves us in the incarnation say about the nature of divine power? That is, how may such an understanding of power affect the way we serve and engage in mission?

4. What is the importance of perichoresis to the way we understand the movement of the triune life of God? How may the perichoretic notion of "indwelling" or "dancing/movement" influence the way we carry out ministry or worship God? Explain the implications.

5. How does life in the triune God ground the Wesleyan understanding of social holiness? That is, how does the Trinity make social holiness possible? What are some of the dangers or challenges to the life of social holiness in the church and in society today?

nine

The Praise of the Saints

To confess the triune God is to proclaim and praise this One. Confession, after all, is a public claim of belief. Therefore, the Creed begins appropriately: "We believe." When we as Christians say "God is," we are participating in a holy activity: the sanctifying or hallowing of space and time through the mechanism of holy speech.[1] Christians intentionally earmark certain activities, speech practices, postures, and moments as set apart on account of and directed to the Trinity. Simply put, Trinitarianism and worship go hand in hand.

This link between the Trinity and worship is an important one. As we have already noted in this text, some of the most important rationales for Trinitarianism rested on the early church's worship practices. Because Christians worshiped Jesus, they had to rethink monotheism in a way that Jews could not. Furthermore, since salvation was enacted by Christ, he had to be more than simply an inspired figure. Both in terms of creation and salvation, triune mediation and worship require one

1. John Webster registers such claims compellingly in *Holiness*.

another:[2] We receive favor and love from the Father, through the Son, and in the Spirit; we in turn render our praise in the Spirit, on account of the Son's obedience, all for the hallowing of the Father's name. Christians are beneficiaries of this grace and participants in this work as ones who were baptized in the name, under the authority, and into the life of the Father, Son, and Holy Spirit.

Important to note about the Methodist revival is that it originated and was sustained in the context of worship. As noted in the last chapter, the Methodist movement began with the impulse by some young students to grow in holiness through a communally sustained life of piety. Because worship was at the heart of this revival, one can say that its life and ethos operated and flourished out of a Trinitarian dynamic. The point suggests itself in at least a couple of ways.

First, the Wesleyan movement was marked quite significantly by its hymnody. One can make the case that for a doctrine to be truly Methodist, it has to be set to verse and occasionally sung. Poetry and verse are just as important to this theological subtradition as sermon and treatise. This quality is largely due to the productivity and imagination of Charles Wesley, who in 1767 published a collection titled *Hymns on the Trinity*. Remarkable about this work is its way of elaborating complex Trinitarian concerns in memorable turns of phrase. As such, a Trinitarian logic was registered by Wesley both gram-

2. For an illuminating discussion of these themes, see Witvliet, "What to Do with Our Renewed Trinitarian Enthusiasm," esp. 240–41. For a more sustained account of how we participate in Trinitarian worship, see Torrance, *Worship, Community and the Triune God of Grace.*

matically and rhythmically. For instance, the combining of Jewish monotheism and Christ-worship are on display in this stanza:

> The Lord of hosts himself alone
> Worthy to be rever'd we own,
> By earth and heaven ador'd:
> Let all the one true God proclaim,
> Worship the dread Jehovah's name,
> Bow down to Christ the Lord.[3]

The logic of fourth-century Trinitarianism, culminating in the Nicene heritage, can be detected densely and beautifully in the following:

> Not his own will, as Man, to do,
> From heaven the world's Redeemer came:
> But as th' eternal God and true,
> His and his Father's is the same:
> The Son we as his Sire adore,
> The glorious co-eternal Son;
> In will, in nature, and in power,
> The Sender and the Sent are One.[4]

Matters related to the importance of the incarnation, co-inherence, spiritual senses, and eschatological fullness are all registered in Hymn 44:

> He that hath seen th' Incarnate Son,
> All which of Christ was visible,
> Hath seen the Father too, and known
> (What flesh and blood could not reveal)
> Jehovah is in Jesus' name,
> With God substantially the same.

---

3. *Hymns on the Trinity*, Hymn 1.
4. Ibid., Hymn 35.

He hath beheld the Person join'd
To God invisible, supreme,
He doth the Father's nature find
The plenitude divine in Him,
Who hath to all his followers shown
"I and my Father are but One."

Jesus, Thou Son of the Most high,
To me, ev'n me vouchsafe the grace
To see by faith's internal eye,
Jehovah shining in thy face:
Explain the mystery to my heart,
And bid me then in peace depart.

So when Thou dost with clouds appear
In all thy dazzling majesty
These eyes of flesh shall see Thee here,
Without a veil the Godhead see,
My forehead shall thy Name receive,
And glorious I for ever live.

Also, the divinity of the Holy Spirit is registered outright in these hymns:

Come, Holy Ghost, Thou God most high,
Thou everlasting Spirit come,
Our faithful hearts to certify,
And consecrate thine earthly home:
When thou hast seal'd thy blest abode,
Jehovah's mansion we shall be,
A Temple of the Tri-une God;
For all the Godhead is in Thee.[5]

And finally, Charles makes the point to consider the work of the triune God within the economy of both creation and salvation:

5. Ibid., Hymn 58.

Jehovah the Almighty Lord,
Father of Jesus Christ and Ours,
The heavens created by his *Word*,
And by his *Breath* the heavenly powers:
And that essential Spirit Divine
Whom Jesus breathes into his own,
Doth in the new Creation join
With God and his eternal Son.

To Father, Son and Holy Ghost
Be equal adoration given,
Maker of the celestial host,
Maker of the new earth and heaven!
Joint-Authors of our glorious bliss
We soon shall sing the Three in One,
And God beholding as He is
For ever shout around his throne.[6]

These verses and others show the beauty of rich theological understandings set to verse. As such, these hymns, when sung and read, shape sensibilities and intuitions so that Trinitarianism functionally and practically comes through as a mechanism of coherence. For Wesleyans and Methodists of all stripes, their doctrinal heritage involves doxological aesthetics. The beauty of Trinitarian worship and the elegance of Trinitarian theology are both readily available to those attuned to Methodist hymnody.

Second, Wesleyans and Methodists have a rich tradition of emphasizing the spiritual disciplines. John Wesley throughout his life used a number of categories to classify these, but one overarching idea is that they are "means of grace."[7] Wesley was adamant to stress that we do not earn

6. Ibid., Hymn 101.

7. The definitive study here is Knight, *The Presence of God in the Christian Life*.

or fabricate grace; rather, it is freely and mercifully given by the triune God. In fact, for Wesley grace is not just divine favor, as it is typically defined in Protestantism; grace can also be thought of as the very presence of God.[8] If one persists with the latter understanding, then the means of grace are activities by which humans respond to and grow increasingly conformable in knowledge and love to the presence and character of the Trinity so that in a (qualified) sense we can be partakers of the divine essence.[9]

The means of grace help establish the idea that theology is not just something believed cognitively but a lived reality. We are, do, and become what we believe. As humans we do not simply put our faith into practice, but our practice is indicative *and constitutive* of the quality and essence of our faith. Our Christian lives grow and mature only through practice because we come to see and gain knowledge through our bodies, in time and space, and so forth. Theology, then, is a way of life because its object is the source, condition, and end of all. The logic of Trinitarianism makes such a life possible. Whether we celebrate the Lord's Supper, pray, contemplate Scripture, or engage in Christian conferencing, Christians have the assurance that such activities are not meaningless rituals but life-giving practices that are suffused with Trinitarian richness. Essentially, our lives are made possible by the triune God, and this confession alone should inspire nothing less than ongoing praise, the kind that does and will mark the heavenly host for all eternity.

8. See Heitzenrater, "God with Us."

9. For the concise elaboration of the theme within the Wesleyan corpus, see "Means of Grace."

Hail holy, holy, holy Lord,
Whom One in Three we know,
By all thy heavenly host ador'd
By all thy church below!
One undivided Trinity
With triumph we proclaim:
The universe is full of Thee,
And speaks thy glorious name.

Thee, holy Father, we confess,
Thee, holy Son adore,
Thee, Spirit of true holiness,
We worship evermore:
Thine incommunicable right,
Almighty God, receive,
Which angel-quires and saints in light
And saints embodied give.

Three Persons equally Divine
We magnify and love:
And both the quires erelong shall join
To sing thy praise above:
Hail holy, holy, holy Lord,
(Our heavenly song shall be)
Supreme, Essential One ador'd
In co-eternal Three.[10]

10. *Hymns on the Trinity,* Hymn 109.

Questions for Consideration

1. How did the Wesleyan revival and the life of worship reveal the richness of life in the Trinity? How did Wesleyan hymnody both foster and reveal the life of God through the Spirit and in Christ? How did such hymnody shape spiritual sensibilities?

2. What is the role of the spiritual disciplines in the Christian life and in the ministry of the church? How does the Wesleyan emphasis on practicing the "means of grace" both corporately and individually move persons toward growing in knowledge and love of the presence and power of God?

3. How do Wesleyans and Methodists understand the means of grace as being "suffused" with Trinitarian richness? How does such an understanding enrich the Christian life?

4. What are some of the ways Wesleyans and Methodists today may recover or retrieve the richness of the Trinitarian faith of the church? What kinds of practices or attitudes are necessary to such an exercise of recovery? Why are the lives of the saints or those mature in the Christian life crucial to the way the Christian life is understood?

5. What difference does believing in the Trinity make in terms of daily living and relating? What other questions remain that churches or persons may want to ask?

Bibliography

*Quotes from ancient patristic sources are from the *ANF* and *NPNF* First and Second Series, unless otherwise stated

Athanasius. *On the Incarnation*. Translated and edited by a religious of CSMV. Crestwood, NY: St. Vladimir's Seminary Press, 2002.

Campbell, Ted. *John Wesley and Christian Antiquity*. Nashville: Kingswood, 1991.

————. *Methodist Doctrine*. Rev. ed. Nashville: Abingdon, 2011.

————. "'Pure, Unbounded Love': Doctrine about God in Historic Wesleyan Communities." In *Trinity, Community, and Power*, edited by M. Douglas Meeks, 85–109. Nashville: Kingswood, 2000.

Castelo, Daniel. "Perfecting One Another: Friendship and the Moral Implications of Wesley's Small Groups." *Asbury Journal* 64.1 (2009) 4–21.

————. "Unearthing That Which May Have Always Been." In *Theology, Eucharist, and Ministry*, edited by Jason Vickers. Forthcoming.

Coakley, Sarah. "The Trinity and Gender Reconsidered." In *God's Life in Trinity*, edited by Miroslav Volf and Michael Welker, 133–42. Minneapolis: Fortress, 2006.

Colón-Emeric, Edgardo. *Wesley, Aquinas and Christian Perfection*. Waco: Baylor University Press, 2009.

Daly, Mary. *Beyond God the Father*. Boston: Beacon, 1973.

Feuerbach, Ludwig. *Essence of Christianity*. Translated by George Eliot. Buffalo: Prometheus, 1989.

Gavrilyuk, Paul L., and Sarah Coakley, eds. *The Spiritual Senses*. Cambridge: Cambridge University Press, 2012.

Heitzenrater, Richard P. "Grace with Us." In *Grace upon Grace*, edited by Robert K. Johnston, L. Gregory Jones, and Jonathan R. Wilson, 87–109. Nashville: Abingdon, 1999.

————. *Wesley and the People Called Methodists*. Nashville: Abingdon, 1995.

Hurtado, Larry. "Monotheism." In *Dictionary for Theological Interpretation of the Bible*, edited by Kevin J. Vanhoozer, 519–21. Grand Rapids: Baker Academic, 2005.

————. *One God, One Lord*. Edinburgh: T. & T. Clark, 2003.

Kant, Immanuel. "The Conflict of the Faculties." In *Religion and Rational Theology*, translated and edited by Allen W. Wood and George di Giovanni, 233–309. Cambridge Edition of the Works of Immanuel Kant. Cambridge: Cambridge University Press, 1996.

Kelly, J. N. D. *Early Christian Doctrines*. Rev. ed. San Francisco: Harper & Row, 1978.

Kilby, Karen. "Perichoresis and Projection: Problems with Social Doctrines of the Trinity." *New Blackfriars* 81.957 (2000) 432–45.

Knight, Henry H., III. *The Presence of God in the Christian Life*. Metuchen, NJ: Scarecrow, 1992.

LaCugna, Catherine Mowry. *God for Us: The Trinity and Christian Life*. San Francisco: HarperSanFrancisco, 1991.

————. "God in Communion with Us." In *Freeing Theology: The Essentials of Theology in Feminist Perspective*, edited by Catherine Mowry LaCugna, 83–114. San Francisco: HarperSanFrancisco, 1993.

Leithart, Peter J. *Athanasius*. Grand Rapids: Baker Academic, 2011.

Lewis, C. S. *Mere Christianity*. In *The Complete C. S. Lewis*, 5–177. New York: HarperOne, 2007.

Moltmann, Jürgen. *The Trinity and the Kingdom*. Translated by Margaret Kohl. Minneapolis: Fortress, 1993.

O'Collins, Gerald. *The Tripersonal God: Understanding and Interpreting the Trinity*. New York: Paulist, 1999.

Prestige, G. L. *God in Patristic Thought*. London: SPCK, 1952.

Prothero, Stephen. *God Is Not One: The Eight Rival Religions that Run the World—and Why Their Differences Matter*. New York: HarperOne, 2010.

Rahner, Karl. *The Trinity*. Translated by Joseph Donceel. New York: Crossroad, 1998.

Rowe, C. Kavin. "Biblical Pressure and Trinitarian Hermeneutics." *Pro Ecclesia* 11.3 (2002) 295–312.

Schleiermacher, Friedrich. *The Christian Faith*. Edited by H. R. Mackintosh and J. S. Stewart. Edinburgh: T. & T. Clark, 1999.

Tanner, Kathryn. "Trinity." In *The Blackwell Companion to Political Theology*, edited by Peter Scott and William T. Cavanaugh, 319–32. Malden, MA: Blackwell, 2007.

Torrance, James B. *Worship, Community and the Triune God of Grace.* Downers Grove, IL: InterVarsity, 1996.

Volf, Miroslav. "'The Trinity Is Our Social Program': The Doctrine of the Trinity and the Shape of Social Engagement." *Modern Theology* 14.3 (1998) 403–23.

Wainwright, Arthur. *The Trinity in the New Testament.* London: SPCK, 1962.

Wainwright, Geoffrey. "The Doctrine of the Trinity: Where the Church Stands or Falls." *Interpretation* 45.2 (1991) 117–32.

———. "Methodism and the Apostolic Faith." In *What Should Methodists Teach?*, edited by M. Douglas Meeks, 101–17. Nashville: Kingswood, 1990.

Walsh, Brian J., and J. Richard Middleton. *The Transforming Vision: Shaping a Christian World View.* Downers Grove, IL: InterVarsity, 1984.

Webster, John. *Holiness.* Grand Rapids: Eerdmans, 2003.

Wesley, Charles. "Awake, Thou That Sleepest," Sermon 3. In vol. 1 of *The Works of John Wesley*, edited by Albert C. Outler, 142–58. Nashville: Abingdon, 1984.

———. *Hymns on the Trinity.* Facsimile reprint. Madison, NJ: Charles Wesley Society, 1998.

Wesley, John. "The Almost Christian," Sermon 2. In vol. 1 of *The Works of John Wesley*, edited by Albert C. Outler, 131–41. Nashville: Abingdon, 1984.

———. "The Character of a Methodist." In vol. 9 of *The Works of John Wesley*, edited by Rupert E. Davies, 31–46. Nashville: Abingdon, 1989.

———. "Christian Perfection," Sermon 40. In vol. 2 of *The Works of John Wesley*, edited by Albert C. Outler, 97–124. Nashville: Abingdon, 1985.

———. "The Circumcision of the Heart," Sermon 17. In vol. 1 of *The Works of John Wesley*, edited by Albert C. Outler, 398–414. Nashville: Abingdon, 1984.

———. "An Earnest Appeal to Men of Reason and Religion." In vol. 11 of *The Works of John Wesley*, edited by Gerald R. Cragg, 37–94. Nashville: Abingdon, 1989.

———. "The Great Privilege of Those that Are Born of God," Sermon 19. In vol. 1 of *The Works of John Wesley*, edited by Albert C. Outler, 431–43. Nashville: Abingdon, 1984.

———. "Justification by Faith," Sermon 5. In vol. 1 of *The Works of John Wesley*, edited by Albert C. Outler, 181–99. Nashville: Abingdon, 1984.

Bibliography

————. "Letter of August 3, 1771 to Jane Catherine March." In vol. 5 of *The Letters of the Rev. John Wesley*, edited by John Telford, 270-1. London: Epworth, 1931.

————. "Letter to a Roman Catholic." In vol. 3 of *The Letters of the Rev. John Wesley*, edited by John Telford, 7-14. London: Epworth, 1931.

————. "The Means of Grace," Sermon 16. In vol. 1 of *The Works of John Wesley*, edited by Albert C. Outler, 376-97. Nashville: Abingdon, 1984.

————. "The New Birth," Sermon 45. In vol. 2 of *The Works of John Wesley*, edited by Albert C. Outler, 186-201. Nashville: Abingdon, 1985.

————. "On the Trinity," Sermon 55. In vol. 2 of *The Works of John Wesley*, edited by Albert C. Outler, 373-86. Nashville: Abingdon, 1985.

————. *A Plain Account of Christian Perfection*. Kansas City: Beacon Hill, 1966.

————. "Preface to List of Poetical Works." In vol. 14 of *Wesley's Works*, 319-45. Grand Rapids: Baker, 1979.

————. "The Scripture Way of Salvation," Sermon 43. In vol. 2 of *The Works of John Wesley*, edited by Albert C. Outler, 153-69. Nashville: Abingdon, 1985.

————. "Spiritual Worship," Sermon 77. In vol. 3 of *The Works of John Wesley*, edited by Albert C. Outler, 88-102. Nashville: Abingdon, 1986.

————. "Upon Our Lord's Sermon on the Mount, II," Sermon 22. In vol. 1 of *The Works of John Wesley*, edited by Albert C. Outler, 488-509. Nashville: Abingdon, 1984.

————. "Walking by Sight and Walking by Faith," Sermon 119. In vol. 4 of *The Works of John Wesley*, edited by Albert C. Outler, 48-59. Nashville: Abingdon, 1987.

————. "The Witness of the Spirit, I," Sermon 10. In vol. 1 of *The Works of John Wesley*, edited by Albert C. Outler, 267-84. Nashville: Abingdon, 1984.

————. "The Witness of the Spirit, II," Sermon 11. In vol. 1 of *The Works of John Wesley*, edited by Albert C. Outler, 285-98. Nashville: Abingdon, 1984.

Witvliet, John D. "What to Do with Our Renewed Trinitarian Enthusiasm." In *Trinitarian Theology for the Church*, edited by Daniel J. Treier and David Lauber, 237-53. Downers Grove, IL: InterVarsity Academic, 2009.

Yeago, David S. "The New Testament and the Nicene Dogma." In *The Theological Interpretation of Scripture: Classic and Contemporary Readings*, edited by Stephen E. Fowl, 87–100. Malden, MA: Blackwell, 1997.

Young, William Paul. *The Shack: A Novel*. Newbury Park, CA: Windblown, 2007.